SCHOLASTIC

D0507537

Nonfiction Comprehension *Cliffhangers*

by Tom Conklin

Editor: Mela Ottaiano
Cover design: Brian LaRossa
Cover illustration: Mariusz Stawarski
Interior design: Melinda Belter

ISBN-13: 978-0-439-89738-9
ISBN-10: 0-439-89738-6

5 6 7 8 9 10   40   14 13 12 11 10

NEW YORK • TORONTO • LONDON • AUCKLAND • SYDNEY **Teaching**
MEXICO CITY • NEW DELHI • HONG KONG • BUENOS AIRES *Resources*

Contents

Introduction

The hero is in peril . . .

The team is down by a touchdown with a minute left to play . . .

The baffling mystery leaves the brilliant detective stumped . . .

Who doesn't love a cliffhanger? Everyone enjoys a good story that poses questions and has readers eagerly turning the pages.

This collection of stories presents 15 very special cliffhangers. What makes them so special? Every one of them is true!

Not only are these exciting stories of mystery and heroics true but they span the curriculum, providing your students with valuable reading in the content areas.

These cliffhangers are ideal for group reading situations. Each one is prefaced with suggested discussion topics to activate students' prior knowledge, vocabulary lists, follow-up questions to assess student comprehension, and enrichment activities to develop their writing skills. Plus, look at the "Hot Web-Links" section at the end of the Introduction for a list of online resources that will let your students expand their reading experience online.

Now, buckle up and get ready for some of the most amazing-but-true cliffhangers of all time . . .

How to Use the Nonfiction Comprehension Cliffhangers

Here is a suggested lesson-plan template to use with each story:

1. Prereading

- ✔ Provide a photocopy of the story for each participating student.

- ✔ Write the vocabulary words on the board and brainstorm with students to come up with definitions of each word. Use the definitions given on the teaching guide page to direct the discussion. Challenge students to watch for the words as they read.

- ✔ Lead students in the discussion activities suggested before each story to activate prior knowledge.

2. Group Reading

- ✔ Have groups of students read the stories collectively. Let students take turns reading one or two paragraphs aloud as the rest read along silently. Encourage students to visualize the story's settings, characters, and actions as they read.

- ✔ As individual students finish reading paragraphs aloud, you may wish to apply the "cliffhanger" prediction strategy (see the next page) by asking students to briefly describe what they think is going to happen next in the story.

3. The Cliffhanger

✔ As students reach the Cliffhanger for each story, lead a discussion on what has happened in the story so far. Encourage students to summarize. Have students infer what will happen next based on what they have read to that point. Invite each student to make a prediction. If students disagree, have individual students defend their predictions by citing information in the story.

✔ After students have made their predictions, have them read The Rest of the Story section for each story.

4. Follow-Up/Assessment

✔ Ask students the Talk About It question(s) provided for each story.

✔ Review the vocabulary words for each story. Ask students if they would revise their definitions after reading the words in the context. Encourage students to use a dictionary to find the definition for each word.

✔ Provide students with the URLs from the Hot Web-Links section below in order to extend their "cliffhanger" experience online.

✔ Have students complete the Write About It enrichment activity provided for each story.

Hot Web-Links

Special Note: Please keep in mind that Internet locations and content can change over time. Be sure to preview each Web site first to determine if its intended content is still available and appropriate for the level of your students.

THE BROWN BOMBER
http://www.pbs.org/wgbh/amex/fight/index.html
"The Fight," an episode of the PBS series *The American Experience*, focuses on the Louis-Schmeling bouts. The supporting Web site contains background information on Louis and Schmeling along with loads of source material, including vintage radio broadcasts of both boxing matches.
(You can also find films of the Louis-Schmeling bouts on the site youtube.com. Simply type "schmeling" in the search field there.)

BREAKING THE BARRIER
chuckyeager.org
An in-depth profile of Chuck Yeager's career, including film clips of the Bell X-1 in flight and an audio clip in which Yeager recounts his historic flight in his own words.

SCHOOLS: BLACK AND WHITE
http://www.nps.gov/brvb/index.htm
The official Web site for the Brown v. Board of Education National Historic Site. The Historic Site is housed in the old Monroe School, which Linda Brown was forced to attend. The Web site includes fascinating multimedia background material on the case.

GOING FOR THE GOLD
http://www.strug.org
Kerri Strug's official Web site contains lots of personal information, along with Kerri's own perspective on her efforts to achieve Olympic success.

Hot Web-Links (continued)

SCOTT OF THE ANTARCTIC
http://www.antarcticconnection.com
An excellent site providing information on weather and wildlife on Antarctica (including the current temperature at the South Pole). It also has a good section on Antarctic exploration, including an overview of Scott and Amundsen.

ON TOP OF THE WORLD
http://www.achievement.org/autodoc/page/ hil0pro-1
The Academy of Achievement Web site provides an excellent in-depth profile of Sir Edmund, along with photos from his historic climb of Mount Everest.

JANE OF THE APES
http://www.janegoodall.com
The Web site of the Jane Goodall Institute, it presents a great deal of material on Goodall's life and work, with many resources for students and teachers.

THE SPECKLED MONSTER
http://www.jennermuseum.com
An in-depth look at Jenner's life and career presented by the charitable trust that maintains a museum in the Jenner family home.

NOVA: EINSTEIN'S BIG IDEA
http://www.pbs.org/wgbh/nova/einstein/
"Einstein's Big Idea," an episode of the PBS series *Nova*, presents loads of background information on Einstein, his theory of relativity, and the theory's impact on the world.

THE MYSTERY OF THE MESSY DESK
http://www.pbs.org/wgbh/aso/tryit/doctor/
Doctor Over Time, an activity from the PBS series *A Science Odyssey*, gives students an interactive chance to see how medicine has improved since 1900, including the development of antibiotics. This Web site also provides a brief biography of Alexander Fleming.

TWO GUYS NAMED STEVE
www.apple.com
Check out the latest innovations from the company founded by Steve Jobs and Steve Wozniak by visiting Apple's home page.

THE STRANGE CASE OF THE FAIRY PHOTOS
http://www.cottingley.net/fairies.shtml
Cottingley.net, the Web site of the town of Cottingley, presents the story of the Cottingley Fairies, including the faked photos and pictures of the locations and people surrounding the controversy.

MARS ATTACKS!
http://jeff560.tripod.com/wotw.html
This Web site, dedicated to "The War of the Worlds" broadcast, presents transcripts of news reports on the broadcast and panic, a link to the show's scripts, and some interesting book excerpts on the event.
(You can also hear a complete mp3 of the broadcast here: http://www.thomasamckean.com /otr/War%20of%20the%20Worlds.mp3)

THE GREATEST FISH STORY EVER TOLD
http://www.pbs.org/wgbh/nova/fish/
"Ancient Creature of the Deep," an episode of PBS's *Nova*, looked at the coelacanth and its discovery in 1938. The Web site supporting the episode is full of great information on the fish and the story of its discovery, including copies of all the letters between Marjorie Courtenay-Latimer and Dr. J. L. B. Smith.

"THE PLAY"
http://alumni.berkeley.edu/KCAA_Multimedia/ theplay_long.ram
The University of California's alumni Web site features two videos of "The Play." The shorter version shows only the kickoff itself. The longer version includes Stanford's great last-minute comeback drive, which set up "The Play."

The Brown Bomber

Curriculum Connections: Social Studies, Physical Education

African American Joe Louis, born in poverty in the segregated South and raised in industrial Detroit, becomes the world's greatest boxer in the 1930s. When German Max Schmeling defeats Joe, Nazi propagandists claim this proves the superiority of the white race. Joe Louis then soundly defeats Schmeling in a rematch.

The Cliffhanger: Joe Louis, humiliated by Max Schmeling in their first fight, takes the ring for their rematch. Can he defeat Schmeling and reclaim the world championship?

Answer: Louis knocks Schmeling out in the first round, proving his earlier defeat was a fluke.

Activating Prior Knowledge

Have students who have seen a boxing match or movies about boxing describe what happens in a bout.

Have students who are familiar with World War II talk about the conflict. Ask what they know about Germany's Nazi regime. Elicit that Nazi Germany was a racist state which believed that whites are a "master race" and have a right to rule the earth, and that the United States fought the Nazis, defeating them and their ideology.

VOCABULARY WORDS
• • • • • • • • •

amateur a person who does something for love, not money

canvas thick fabric, used as the surface of a boxing ring

cautiously carefully, watchfully

confronted to have come face to face with

peppered to be hit with a series of small blows

propaganda untrustworthy information spread to promote a cause

superior to be better than

Talk About It

☞ Why did Joe Louis lose to Max Schmeling in their first fight? *(Joe did not train hard for the fight, Max did. Also, Max studied Joe's boxing style and found a weakness.)*

☞ Why did so many people around the world pay such close attention to the rematch between Joe and Max? *(The Nazis were using the fight in their propaganda.)*

Write About It

✍ Create a poster to promote the rematch between Joe Louis and Max Schmeling. Be sure to include the fight's date and place. Also include slogans to highlight why the fight is sure to be exciting.

The Brown Bomber

Joseph Louis Barrow was a powerful man.

Joe was born in Chambers County, Alabama, on May 13, 1914. His father was a poor farmer named Munroe Barrow, who died when Joe was only 4 years old. Joe's mother, Lillie, washed clothes to earn the money to feed Joe and his seven brothers and sisters. When Joe was 7 years old, his mother married a man named Patrick Brooks, who had eight children of his own. Soon, Lillie and Patrick took their 16 kids and left the farms of Alabama. The family moved north to the big city of Detroit.

Life was hard for Joe and his family. When he was 12 years old, Joe got his first jobs. Before going to school he worked in Detroit's Eastern Market, selling fruits and vegetables. After school, Joe delivered huge blocks of ice for people to use in their ice boxes. Joe later said that hauling 50-pound blocks of ice built up his muscles. He would put that strength to good use.

Joe's mother had dreams that her son would be a musician. She gave him money for violin lessons. But Joe wasn't a very good musician. Instead, he loved the thrills and challenges of boxing. So Joe used the money to rent a locker at the Brewster Recreation Center, where boxers trained. After a few weeks, Joe's violin teacher came to his house, looking for him. That night, Joe's mother confronted Joe. At first, she was mad because he had been sneaking behind her back. But after Joe told her how much he loved boxing, she gave in. "Whatever you do, Joe, just give it your best," she said.

Joe began fighting amateur matches as a teenager. Before one of his first fights, Joe had to fill out some forms. Joe wrote his first and middle names in the blank. There wasn't enough space for him to add his last name, Barrow. So from that moment on, Joe Barrow was known as Joe Louis.

At first, Joe won some fights and lost some fights. He took a job building cars at Ford Motors. But he never gave up. Joe found good trainers, who taught him how to use his strength in the ring. By the time he was 20 years old, Joe had fought 58 bouts, and won 54 of them. He decided it was time to turn pro.

Once he turned pro, Joe became a star. He worked very hard and fought every chance he got. He earned only $50 in his first fight. But a year and a half later, Joe had won more than $370,000—back when the average yearly salary was only $1,250! Joe won his first 27 bouts—23 of them by knockouts. People began calling him "the Brown Bomber." One sportswriter wrote that Joe was "the greatest fighter of all time." People said that Joe Louis was unbeatable. American boxers were afraid to fight him.

Nonfiction Comprehension Cliffhangers © 2008 by Tom Conklin, Scholastic Teaching Resources

One fighter, though, was eager to take on Joe Louis.

Max Schmeling was the European champion. Born in Germany on September 28, 1905, Max was almost as big as Joe Louis. He also worked as hard as Joe. But Max didn't have Joe's speed or strength. When it was announced that Max Schmeling was going to fight Joe Louis, no one thought Max stood a chance.

Max worked hard to prepare for the fight. He trained hard. And he studied movies of Joe's fights. He noticed that Joe lowered his guard after throwing a jab. Max planned to take advantage of that weakness.

Joe, on the other hand, didn't work very hard to prepare for the fight. He played golf every day, even though his trainers told him that a good golf swing wouldn't help him in the ring. Still, Joe was confident that he would beat Max.

Joe Louis and Max Schmeling got into the ring on June 19, 1936. The fight took place in Yankee Stadium. People were certain that Joe would beat Max. Many of the seats were empty. No one was expecting much of a fight.

That night, Max Schmeling shocked Joe Louis—and the world.

For the first three rounds, Max and Joe fought cautiously. But in the fourth round, Joe threw a jab and lowered his guard for a split second. Max pounced, landing a hard punch on Joe's chin. Joe staggered, then fell. He managed to get back to his feet and go on. But after the fourth round, Max took over the fight. Every time Joe lowered his guard, Max was ready. He rocked Joe with 91 hard punches with his right hand. In the 12th round, Max Schmeling knocked out Joe Louis.

Americans were stunned. They were certain that Joe Louis would beat Schmeling. People in Germany were surprised, too. And some very, very evil people were happy to see Joe Louis get knocked out.

Three years before Max beat Joe, Adolf Hitler had become the leader of Germany. Hitler and his supporters in the Nazi party were racists. They thought that black people were inferior to white people. Seeing Max Schmeling beat Joe Louis, they claimed that it proved that their views were correct. They used the fight as propaganda. "Schmeling knocks out the negro," wrote one Nazi leader. "Wonderful . . . the white man defeats the black man, and the white man is a German!"

After the fight, Joe learned a lesson. He would never again take an opponent lightly.

A year later, Joe Louis beat James J. Braddock to win the heavyweight title. After he became champion, Joe fought anyone who wanted a shot at the title. Even though he beat anyone who fought him, there was one fighter Joe wanted to take on: Max Schmeling.

Nonfiction Comprehension Cliffhangers © 2008 by Tom Conklin, Scholastic Teaching Resources

A rematch between Joe and Max was scheduled. They were to fight exactly two years after their first battle, on June 22, 1938.

As Joe and Max climbed into the ring that night, Yankee Stadium was packed. In one corner stood Joe Louis—a poor American, born in a shack, who through hard work and dedication had become the top fighter in the world. In the other corner was the great German, Max Schmeling, backed by Nazi Germany. The Nazis said that the first fight showed that white people were superior to black people. If Schmeling beat Joe Louis for a second time, they claimed that it would prove once and for all that the Nazis were right.

People all over the world listened to the fight over the radio. As the opening bell rang, and Joe and Max skipped into the ring, fists raised, ready to fight. Who would win? America's Brown Bomber, or Hitler's favorite fighter? The world held its breath . . .

Who do you think won this battle? Turn the page to see if you were right!

The Brown Bomber

the rest of the story

In the first fight, it took Max Schmeling 12 rounds to knock out Joe Louis. The rematch didn't last nearly as long!

Joe Louis came out swinging. He was in peak condition and peppered Max Schmeling with punches. Two minutes and four seconds into the fight, Joe hit Max with a powerful punch. Max dropped to the canvas and did not get up. Joe Louis won the rematch with a first-round knockout!

Years later, Joe remembered the fight. "I had nothing personally against Max, but in my mind, I wasn't champion until I beat him," Joe said. "The rest of it—black against white—was somebody's talk. I had nothing against the man, except I had to beat him for myself."

Nonfiction Comprehension Cliffhangers © 2008 by Tom Conklin, Scholastic Teaching Resources

Breaking the Barrier

Curriculum Connections: Science, Social Studies

Chuck Yeager, an American pilot born and raised in rural West Virginia, becomes a war hero and test pilot. He is the first person ever to fly faster than the speed of sound.

The Cliffhanger: Chuck Yeager flies the experimental Bell X-1 rocket plane in an attempt to break the sound barrier, despite having a set of broken ribs. Will he succeed?

Answer: Yeager breaks the sound barrier.

Activating Prior Knowledge

Tell students that sound travels in waves through the air in our atmosphere. Ask students how quickly they think sound travels. Discuss how light moves much faster than sound. Tell them that thunder and lightning occur at the same time and place, but that we see the lightning before we hear the thunder, since light travels faster than sound. Scientists can precisely measure the speed of sound. Under normal conditions, sound travels at 761 miles per hour. Ask students to imagine traveling at speeds greater than that. Tell them they are about to read about the first person to "break the sound barrier" by traveling faster than the speed of sound.

Ask students if they know anything about World War II. Have them describe the conflict in their own words.

VOCABULARY WORDS
• • • • • • • • •

altitude distance from the ground

conquer to win, as at war

coordinated to be physically agile and skilled

engineers people trained in designing and building machines

engines machines that convert energy into motion

experimental something undergoing a test

invaded to enter forcefully as an enemy

propeller a set of blades that spin in order to propel an airplane or a boat

stationed when a soldier, sailor, or pilot is assigned to stay someplace

veterinarian a doctor trained to care for animals

Talk About It

☞ How did his experiences growing up help prepare Chuck Yeager for his success as a pilot? *(He developed his eye-hand coordination, learned how engines and machines work, and learned good work habits.)*

Write About It

✍ Write a poem describing the first flight to break the sound barrier.

Breaking the Barrier

Hamlin, West Virginia, is a tiny town far from any big cities.
One boy who grew up there, Chuck Yeager, loved Hamlin
and the slow pace of life there. Little did Chuck know that he
would one day be the fastest human being on the planet.

Chuck Yeager was born February 13, 1923, in Myra, West Virginia. Myra wasn't even a town. It was just a post office on a stream called Mud River. Chuck's family moved to the town of Hamlin when he was a young boy.

Chuck was a typical boy in small-town America. He did all right in school, but would rather go fishing or explore the woods than study. He was good at sports—football and basketball were his favorites. In fifth grade, Chuck had to give a book report on a story called "Crooked Bill." Later in his life, Chuck would say that giving that book report was the hardest thing he had ever done!

His father taught young Chuck many valuable lessons. Most important, Chuck was taught to work hard and to never give up. "My father taught me to finish anything I started," Chuck said.

Even as a boy, Chuck worked with tools. He liked to take engines apart and put them back together again. He was also a great student in his high school typing class. "Anything that took hand-eye coordination, I had a good time at it," Chuck said.

The world Chuck Yeager grew up in was very different from today's world. Back then, there was no television or Internet. Airplanes were very rare. Chuck was a teenager before he even saw one. A small airplane flying over Hamlin had to make an emergency landing in a cornfield about a mile from Chuck's house. Chuck heard about it and rode his bicycle to see the plane. "I wasn't impressed," he recalled. He got back on his bike and rode back home.

While Chuck grew up in Hamlin, things were happening far away that would change his life—and the world—forever.

Throughout the 1930s, Germany was ruled by Adolf Hitler and the Nazi party. Hitler came to power planning to conquer the rest of Europe. To that end, Hitler and the Nazis built a giant army. The Germans made the world's fastest, most dangerous war planes. They knew that if their airplanes controlled the skies, then the German army could conquer their enemies.

Leaders in the United States and Europe saw the threat of the Nazis. The United States began to build up its own military to stop the Germans. The

Nonfiction Comprehension Cliffhangers © 2008 by Tom Conklin, Scholastic Teaching Resources

U.S. Army built its air force, making fast, agile planes that could do battle with the German air force.

Chuck Yeager graduated from high school in 1941. By then, Germany had already invaded its neighbors and started World War II. It was clear that the United States would soon be part of the war. Chuck, like many other men and women his age, signed up to fight for the United States.

Chuck joined the U.S. Army Air Forces in the fall of 1941. For the first time, he left West Virginia. Chuck headed to California, where he became a mechanic working on airplanes. "It was easy for me," Chuck said, "because I had already had so much experience in mechanical things, like engines." Chuck enjoyed his work, but wondered if there was more he could do to help win the war.

One day, Chuck saw a notice on a bulletin board, inviting regular soldiers to sign up for pilot's training. Although Chuck had never been in an airplane in his life, he signed up. Chuck was accepted in the program. He would never forget the first time he flew in a plane—Chuck got sick and threw up!

Despite getting sick his first time in a plane, Chuck soon proved to be one of the most skilled pilots in the U.S. Army. With other American pilots, he was stationed in England. From there, they would fly small, quick fighter planes on long trips over Europe and into Germany.

As a fighter pilot, Chuck had many hair-raising adventures. On his second trip, Chuck was shot down over France. He survived by parachuting from his plane and making his way back to England. On another trip, Chuck single-handedly shot down five German fighters. By the end of the war, Chuck was one of the top pilots in the world.

Chuck came home from the war a hero. He married his high school sweetheart, a young woman named Glennis. Chuck signed up to be an Air Force test pilot. That meant he would be the first person to fly experimental airplanes. It is a tricky, very dangerous job. Chuck loved it.

In the years after World War II, engineers worked to develop faster planes. The planes Chuck Yeager flew in the war all had propeller engines. The newest planes were using jet engines, which make planes fly much, much faster. Before jets could travel at their top speeds, though, engineers had to solve a puzzle—how to design a plane that could break the "sound barrier."

The sound barrier refers to the speed of sound. Sound waves travel through the air at a speed of about 761 miles per hour. As jet planes flew faster and approached that speed, problems sprang up. A plane traveling near the speed of sound would have great air pressure build up on its wings. The plane would become impossible to control. For a time, some engineers

Nonfiction Comprehension Cliffhangers © 2008 by Tom Conklin, Scholastic Teaching Resources

thought that it would be impossible for a plane to travel faster than the speed of sound.

Chuck and Glennis moved to California, where Chuck worked with engineers designing new airplanes. One plane Chuck would fly was called the Bell X-1. It didn't have a jet engine—the Bell X-1 was powered by a rocket! The plane wasn't able to take off from the ground on its own. Instead, it would be strapped to the bottom of a giant plane. The big plane would fly the Bell X-1 to a high altitude. There, the Bell X-1 would be dropped from the plane. As it fell away, the pilot would turn on the rocket engine—and the Bell X-1 would shoot off like a bullet.

Chuck was scheduled to fly the Bell X-1 on October 14, 1947. Two days before, Chuck and Glennis went for a horseback ride. Chuck, chasing Glennis across the desert, fell off his horse. The next day, Chuck was in great pain. He went to the only doctor around who was not in the army—a local veterinarian. The vet gave Chuck the bad news. He had two broken ribs.

Chuck swore his wife to secrecy. He knew that if his bosses knew about his ribs, they would have another pilot fly the Bell X-1. Chuck was determined to break the sound barrier himself.

On October 14, Chuck got onboard the huge plane with the smaller Bell X-1 strapped to its belly. As the two planes climbed to 20,000 feet, Chuck hid a sawed-off broomstick under his jacket. Soon, it was time to launch the rocket plane.

Chuck climbed into the Bell X-1. Once in the cockpit, Chuck took out the short broomstick. He used it as a lever to seal the hatch. Because of his injured ribs, it would hurt too much to shut the hatch by hand.

Sitting in the cockpit, Chuck went over his list of things to do during the flight. Minutes later, the big plane went into a dive to build up speed. Finally, the giant plane pulled out of its dive. The straps holding the Bell X-1 snapped away. The little rocket plane dropped off into space. In the cockpit, Chuck blinked. The sunlight was blinding as the Bell X-1 fell from the shadow of the larger plane.

Chuck Yeager, his broken ribs aching, reached out for the switches to ignite the rocket. "If you're going to blow up, this is when it's going to happen," Chuck once said. One hand gripping the plane's controls, Chuck tossed the first switch . . .

What do you think happened next? Make a prediction. Then turn the page to see what happened to Chuck Yeager and the Bell X-1.

Nonfiction Comprehension Cliffhangers © 2008 by Tom Conklin, Scholastic Teaching Resources

Breaking the Barrier

the rest of the story

The rocket engine roared to life, and the Bell X-1 shot across the sky like lightning. In the plane's cockpit, Chuck Yeager was pinned to his seat, feeling pressure equal to three times his normal weight. Despite the pain of his broken ribs, Chuck kept control of the plane. He headed straight up. "I aimed for the dark part of the sky," Chuck remembers.

As the Bell X-1 soared faster up into the sky, the controls bucked in Chuck's hand. The plane began to shake, as pressure built up on its wings. Just below the speed of sound, the plane shook violently. Chuck pulled slightly on the controls, and the plane's flight smoothed out. He studied the controls—as the plane zoomed past 761 miles per hour, a loud "boom" echoed through the sky. Chuck Yeager had broken the sound barrier!

"You don't really think about the outcome of any kind of flight," Chuck says, "because you really don't have any control over it. You concentrate on what you are doing, to do the best job you are doing."

Chuck had learned the lesson his father had taught him so many years before—work hard, and always finish a job you have started.

Nonfiction Comprehension Cliffhangers © 2008 by Tom Conklin, Scholastic Teaching Resources

Schools: Black and White

Curriculum Connections: Social Studies

Young Linda Brown's desire to go to her neighborhood school sparks the landmark lawsuit Brown v. Board of Education, *which resulted in segregation being declared illegal throughout the United States.*

The Cliffhanger: Having heard both sides of the argument, the U.S. Supreme Court must decide whether or not to uphold a law that declares "separate but equal" schools to be legal.

Answer: The Supreme Court unanimously declares "separate but equal" to be illegal.

Activating Prior Knowledge

Ask students to imagine a world where black and white people are not allowed to eat together, work together, or even go to school together. Discuss whether or not it would be fair for one race to make it illegal for the other race to use certain restaurants, theaters, or schools. Define such laws as segregation. Then point out that segregation was the law in much of the United States only 50 years ago.

Talk About It

☞ What evidence did Thurgood Marshall use to prove that "separate but equal" schools were not fair? *(Experiments by social scientists in which African American students from segregated schools chose black dolls as "bad.")*

☞ How many of the Supreme Court justices sided with Chief Justice Warren in finding "separate but equal" schools to be unequal? *(All of them—it was a unanimous 9–0 decision.)*

Write About It

✐ Imagine you live in a town where black and white people are forced to go to separate schools, restaurants, and stores. Write a letter to the editor of the local newspaper expressing your views on the subject.

VOCABULARY WORDS
• • • • • • • • •

conclude to decide or settle

doctrine a belief or system of beliefs accepted as true

inherently basically, naturally

justify to show to be just or right

precedent an act or decision that serves to guide or justify later acts or decisions

reputation the general opinion that the public has of someone

inferior of a lesser quality or value

unanimously in complete agreement

Schools: Black and White

All Linda Brown wanted was to go to school with her friends.

It was the fall of 1951, and Linda was about to start the third grade. She lived in Topeka, Kansas, only seven blocks from Sumner Elementary School. The Topeka school district, though, said that Linda had to go to Monroe School. To get to that school, Linda had to walk six blocks to a bus stop, then ride a bus to another part of town. It seemed silly to go all of that way, when Sumner School was so close. Besides, Linda's friends from the neighborhood all went to Sumner School.

One morning early in the school year, Linda's father, Oliver, walked with Linda to Sumner School. Oliver Brown wanted to talk to the principal. Oliver thought that he might talk the principal into letting Linda go to the local school. "When I found out that day that I might be able to go to [Sumner] School, I was just thrilled," Linda later said.

Linda sat near the school secretary while her father met with the principal. After a few minutes, she heard her father raise his voice. Oliver Brown was arguing with the school principal. "Then he immediately came out of the office, took me by the hand, and we walked home from the school," Linda remembered. "I just couldn't understand what was happening because I was so sure that I was going to go to school with all of my playmates."

What Oliver Brown heard from the principal made him angry. The school system would not allow Linda Brown to attend her neighborhood school. Why? Because Linda Brown was African American. And African Americans were not allowed in the same school as white kids!

Neither Linda nor her father knew it at the time, but their visit to Sumner School that day would change the course of American history.

Rules like the one that said Linda could not go to her local school used to be common in the United States. In much of the country, segregation was the law. Segregation is the practice of separating people because of their race. In a segregated society, black people and white people cannot go to the same schools, eat in the same restaurants, or even use the same bathrooms.

Segregation started in the United States in the years after the Civil War. The war had ended slavery in our country, but many people still did not want to treat African Americans as full citizens. Many states passed laws segregating black and white Americans. This meant African Americans living

Nonfiction Comprehension Cliffhangers © 2008 by Tom Conklin, Scholastic Teaching Resources

in those states had to go to separate schools, restaurants, theaters, stores, hotels . . . everything.

Right from the start of segregation, African Americans challenged laws that separated blacks and whites. In 1896, an African American named Homer Plessy had bought a first-class ticket on a railroad car. The train's conductor told Plessy to move to the "black" car at the back of the train. When Plessy wouldn't budge, he was kicked off the train and thrown into prison. Plessy took his case all the way to the Supreme Court. The Supreme Court is the last word on the law in the United States. The court listened to both sides of the case, and decided that Homer Plessy deserved to go to prison. The Supreme Court ruled that it was all right to force African Americans to use separate facilities, as long as the facilities were "equal." For decades after that, the phrase "separate but equal" was used to justify segregation laws.

In 1951, when the Topeka schools would not let Linda Brown go to her neighborhood school, her father Oliver decided to fight back. Oliver Brown went to the local branch of a group called the National Association for the Advancement of Colored People (NAACP). The NAACP had been working for years to get the Supreme Court to reverse, or change, the *Plessy v. Ferguson* decision. The NAACP had already decided to fight the idea of "separate but equal" schools. The lawyer in charge of the NAACP's case was a brilliant young man named Thurgood Marshall.

Finally, in 1952, *Brown v. Board of Education* was put on the list of cases that the Supreme Court would hear. Marshall told the justices of the Supreme Court that it was impossible for schools to be "separate but equal." Such laws, he argued, were like saying that African Americans "are inferior to all other human beings."

Marshall showed the court the results of experiments by social scientists. In the experiments, young African Americans who went to segregated schools were given black dolls and white dolls. They were asked which dolls were "bad." Most of the kids picked the black dolls. The black kids who went to segregated schools did not think they were equal to other kids.

Finally, in 1954, the justices of the Supreme Court announced that they were going to decide the case of *Brown v. Board of Education.* It wasn't clear how the court would look at the case. Why? There was a brand new chief justice of the Supreme Court named Earl Warren.

Warren, a Republican, had never been a judge before he joined the Supreme Court. Before that, he had been governor of California. He had been a strict law-and-order leader. On the other hand, Warren was also known as being a broad-minded man. He was always willing to hear both sides of an argument.

Nonfiction Comprehension Cliffhangers © 2008 by Tom Conklin, Scholastic Teaching Resources

On May 17, 1954, Thurgood Marshall and the other NAACP lawyers climbed the marble steps of the Supreme Court to hear the court decision. They hoped that Earl Warren and the other justices had been open to their arguments.

Marshall and the other members of his legal team stood at attention as the nine justices, looking regal in their black robes, took their places on the court's bench. The clerk of the court announced that the Supreme Court had reached a decision. Thurgood Marshall held his breath as Earl Warren himself began to read the decision . . .

What do you think happened next? In 1954, did the Supreme Court say that "separate but equal" could remain the law of the land? Or would school segregation become illegal? Make a prediction. Then turn the page to find out how the Supreme Court decided the case of Brown v. Board of Education.

Nonfiction Comprehension Cliffhangers © 2008 by Tom Conklin, Scholastic Teaching Resources

Schools: Black and White

the rest of the story

Chief Justice Earl Warren looked stern as he read. First, Warren restated the arguments both sides had made. Finally, he came to the part of his speech where he announced the decision.

"We unanimously conclude that in the field of public education the doctrine 'separate but equal' has no place. Separate educational facilities are inherently unequal."

Thurgood Marshall beamed with pride and joy. He had won the case—"separate but equal" was no longer legal. With that precedent set, all of the other segregations laws were doomed.

It would take decades before the effects of segregation would be reversed. In many ways, we are still living with the effects of "separate but equal." But thanks to the fighting spirit of Oliver and Linda Brown, the legal skills of Thurgood Marshall, and the wisdom of Chief Justice Earl Warren, segregation is no longer legal in the United States.

Nonfiction Comprehension Cliffhangers © 2008 by Tom Conklin, Scholastic Teaching Resources

Going for the Gold

Curriculum Connections: Social Studies, Physical Education

Gymnast Kerri Strug badly twists her ankle during the final event of the 1996 Olympics but comes back to nail her final attempt and win the gold medal.

The Cliffhanger: Kerri Strug, barely able to walk, runs down the mat for her final try at the vault in the 1996 Olympics. She hits the springboard, twists into the air, and . . .

Answer: Kerri lands perfectly before collapsing in pain. Her brave effort wins a gold medal for Kerri and her teammates.

Activating Prior Knowledge

Have students imagine what it would be like to leave their homes and school to practice a sporting event. Tell them they would have to practice seven days a week and give up pizza, ice cream, candy, and other favorite foods. Discuss with students the dedication that would make a kid do something like this.

Have fans of the Olympics describe the gymnastics portion of the games. Elicit that gymnasts participate in a wide variety of events that require a number of different skills.

> ### VOCABULARY WORDS
> • • • • • • • • •
> **agonizing** very painful
> **competed** to have strived against others in a competition
> **gymnast** an athlete who takes part in events showing off strength and agility
> **ligaments** tissue linking muscles to bone
> **massaged** rubbed or kneaded a body part
> **somersault** to tumble forward head over heels
> **splurge** to indulge oneself
> **triumph** a great victory or success

Talk About It

☞ Why did Kerri Strug leave home when she was 13 years old? *(To train in gymnastics with coach Bela Karolyi.)*

☞ Why was there so much pressure on Kerri before she made her final vault in the 1996 Olympics? *(If she did well, she and her teammates would win the gold medal. If she did not, they would not get the gold. Plus, she had injured herself on the previous vault.)*

Write About It

✍ Pick a hero of yours who overcame adversity to accomplish something. Write a song or a rap describing your hero and their achievement.

Nonfiction Comprehension Cliffhangers © 2008 by Tom Conklin, Scholastic Teaching Resources

Going for the Gold

When she was 13 years old, Kerri Strug left home.
She wasn't running away, though. Young Kerri had decided
to give up the comforts of home to go for Olympic gold.

Kerri was born in 1977 and spent her early years in Tucson, Arizona. She was the youngest of three kids. Kerri's sister, Lisa, was a gymnast, and young Kerri wanted to be just like her big sister. When Kerri was only 4 years old, she did flips and somersaults around the house. At an early age she joined her mother in a "Mom and Tot" gymnastics class. No one knew it at the time, but Kerri was already on her way to the Olympics.

Kerri competed in her first gymnastics meet when she was only 8 years old. She did well and went on to compete in other meets. By the time she was 12, Kerri was good enough that she began to seriously dream of competing in the Olympics.

There was one catch. To make it to the Olympics, an athlete must train with a top coach. Unfortunately, there were no world-class gymnastics coaches in Tucson. "I wanted to really go somewhere in gymnastics, so I figured I would have to leave home," Kerri remembers. "And if you're going to leave home, you might as well come to the best."

Fortunately for Kerri, one of the best gymnastics coaches lived and worked in Houston, Texas. The coach's name was Bela Karolyi. The best young gymnasts from around the country would come to train with Karolyi. When Kerri was 13 years old, she and her parents decided she should leave home to work with Coach Karolyi in Texas.

As she trained with Coach Karolyi, Kerri lived with a series of host families. Although her host families were friendly, Kerri still was often homesick. "It was very hard at times," Kerri recalls. "When you got down or had a bad day, you got to a phone and talked to your parents a lot."

There was one thing about working with Coach Karolyi: Kerri did not have much time to be homesick! Kerri worked on her gymnastics eight hours a day, six or seven days a week. Kerri would train for a few hours in the morning, then go to school for three hours. She would then train for many more hours in the afternoon. Kerri would have to find the time for homework at night and on weekends. It was an exhausting schedule.

As she trained hard and got better and better at gymnastics, Kerri had very little time for fun. The only times she took a break was when she visited

Nonfiction Comprehension Cliffhangers © 2008 by Tom Conklin, Scholastic Teaching Resources

Nonfiction Comprehension Cliffhangers © 2008 by Tom Conklin, Scholastic Teaching Resources

an aunt and uncle who lived in Houston. During those visits, Kerri would "splurge" by eating frozen strawberries and staying up late to watch *Saturday Night Live*.

Still, Kerri thought all of the hard work and sacrifices were worth it. When she was only 14 years old, Kerri told an interviewer, "A gymnast's career is pretty short. Most of them will peak at 15 or 16. When I get through with this, I have the rest of my life to do other things."

After training with Coach Karolyi for a year, Kerri tried out for the American Olympics team. As a gymnast, Kerri had to compete in many different events. She did very well in most of them. The tryouts ended with the floor exercise, which was one of Kerri's strongest events. As she performed her routine, disaster struck. Kerri lost her balance and fell. After, Kerri was certain that her mistake would cost her a spot on the team. But when the scores were added up, Kerri was a member of the U.S. women's Olympic gymnastics team. At the age of 14, she would be the youngest athlete to represent the United States in the Olympics that year.

Kerri performed well at the 1992 Olympics, although the experience was both exciting and frustrating. The U.S. women came in third place that year, earning bronze medals. But Kerri did not get to compete in the all-around competition.

After the Olympics, Kerri faced another major challenge. Her coach, Bela Karolyi, decided to retire. Kerri, at the age of 14, was just entering her prime as a gymnast. But now she did not have a coach to help her become the best gymnast she could be.

Over the next three years, Kerri tried working with three different coaches. Each time she changed coaches, Kerri had to move to a different part of the country. But none of these coaches were as good for Kerri as Coach Karolyi had been. Finally after three years, Kerri hurt herself badly in a meet. She tore a muscle, and the doctors told her it would take six months to heal.

Kerri decided to take a break from gymnastics and move back to Tucson. For the first time in many years, Kerri lived like a typical teenager. She went to school on a normal schedule. Although she continued to practice gymnastics, Kerri did not push herself as hard as she had before the '92 Olympics.

In 1995, Kerri graduated from high school. She had worked so hard at her studies that she graduated a year ahead of schedule. Kerri planned to go to college. But one thing stopped her from continuing with her education: Kerri still dreamed of winning a gold medal. And the 1996 Olympics, to be held in Atlanta, were just a year away. "I thought about all the work I put into it," Kerri later remembered, "and I didn't want to blow it after I had gotten so close."

Meanwhile, Kerri's former coach, Bela Karolyi, had begun coaching again. Kerri decided to take one more shot at Olympic gold. She put off going to college and went to train with Coach Karolyi.

Kerri worked harder than ever as she prepared for the Olympics. In March 1996, she won a gold medal at the America's Cup gymnastics competition. Her confidence soared. On June 30, Kerri easily earned a spot on the U.S. women's Olympic team at the Olympic tryouts in Boston. In July, Kerri and the rest of the team headed to Atlanta for the 1996 Olympic Games.

The American women's gymnastics team that year was one of the best ever. People called them "the Magnificent Seven." The American women had never won a gold medal in the team competition, which had been won by the Russians many times. The year 1996 seemed to be the one in which the Americans might finally win a gold medal.

On the final day of the competition, the Americans and Russians were neck and neck. Forty thousand spectators crammed into the Georgia Dome to see which team would win the gold medal. The last event was the vault. In this event, gymnasts sprint down a track, jump off a springboard, and spring over a tall table called a vaulting horse. Gymnasts are scored by how gracefully they move and how difficult their jumps are.

As the teams prepared for the vault, everyone in the Georgia Dome knew that the Americans needed at least one top score if they were going to win the gold medal. The American gymnast before Kerri had bad luck. She stumbled and fell on both of her vaults. Her scores were terrible. That meant it was up to Kerri to perform a perfect vault and win the gold.

Kerri lined up for her first vault. She sprinted down the path, hit the springboard, and flipped over the vault. As she came down, Kerri crumpled to the mat in pain. The crowd gasped. Kerri had twisted her ankle! As she hobbled off the mat, it looked as if Kerri could hardly walk, much less take her last run at the vault.

The crowd grew hushed as Kerri massaged and stretched her ankle. After a few agonizing moments, Kerri limped to the end of the path. She would finish the event!

The crowd held its breath as Kerri lined up for her final shot at Olympic gold. Ignoring the terrible pain in her ankle, Kerri ran down the path to the springboard and vault . . .

What happened next? Did Kerri Strug overcome her injury to win the medal? Or did she fail in a valiant effort? Make a prediction. Then turn the page to see if you were correct.

Nonfiction Comprehension Cliffhangers © 2008 by Tom Conklin, Scholastic Teaching Resources

Going for the Gold

the rest of the story

Kerri Strug hit the springboard at full speed and soared into the air. She put her hands on the vault, then twisted gracefully in the air and came down on the far side . . .

And landed perfectly! Her vault was beautiful and earned a top score of 9.712. Kerri pumped her arms in triumph, then collapsed to the mat in agony. Her coach, Bela Karolyi, rushed onto the mat and carried her off as the crowd cheered.

As it turned out, Kerri had torn two ligaments in her ankle—yet still landed a tremendous vault.

After years of effort, sacrifice, and bravery, Kerri Strug had truly earned her gold medal.

Scott of the Antarctic

Curriculum Connections: Social Studies, Geography

British explorer Robert Falcon Scott leads a group of men on an expedition across Antarctica in hopes of being the first people to visit the South Pole.

The Cliffhanger: As they approach the South Pole, Scott and his men see something shocking. What?

Answer: Scott and the others find a flag already at the pole. Another group of explorers had beaten them there.

Activating Prior Knowledge

Ask students which of the seven continents has the smallest population. If none of them answer "Antarctica," remind them that Antarctica is one of the continents, and that it has no native population. Only a handful of scientists live there. Have a student find Antarctica on a globe. Tell students that Antarctica has a bitterly cold climate. The temperature never goes above freezing and is usually well below zero degrees Fahrenheit. Ninety-five percent of Antarctica is covered with ice. No large land animals live there. There are no towns or cities. And Antarctica is larger than the 48 contiguous United States and Mexico combined. Ask students to imagine crossing such a harsh place—on foot! Tell them they are about to read the story of explorers who tried to do just that.

Talk About It

☞ For how many years did Scott work in his attempt to make it to the South Pole? *(Almost 12.)*

Write About It

✍ What is your dream? Write a paragraph describing a goal you would spend more than ten years working to achieve.

VOCABULARY WORDS
• • • • • • • • •

expedition a journey or voyage made for a specific purpose

exploration the investigation of unknown regions

military having to do with war or the Armed Forces

predilection tending to think favorably of someone or something

preposterous going against nature or common sense

trek a long journey

trudged to have walked wearily

volunteers people who offer to do a task

FOR THE TEACHER

Scott of the Antarctic

On a sunny day in June of 1899, the chance meeting of two friends would launch one of the greatest adventure stories of the twentieth century.

That summer day, a young naval officer named Robert Falcon Scott was walking in London. He stopped when he saw a familiar face across the street. It was Sir Clements Markham, who was the head of the Royal Geographic Society. Sir Clements had met Scott many years before, and Scott admired the older man. Scott called out to Sir Clements, and crossed the street to say hello. Sir Clements was glad to see Scott. As they were near his house, Sir Clements invited Scott in for a chat. By the time Scott came out of Sir Clements's house, his life had changed. Sir Clements had told Scott about the Royal Geographic Society's Antarctic expedition.

In 1899, Great Britain was maybe the most powerful nation on earth. The British had explored just about every corner of the world. In fact, by 1899, there were very few places on the planet that had not been explored. But there were two great blank spots left on the map. No one had yet made it to the North Pole or the South Pole. Whichever nation sent the first explorers to "claim" the poles would score a big victory in public opinion.

Sir Clements Markham explained all of this to Robert Scott that sunny June day. He also told Scott that the Royal Geographic Society was raising the money to send a team of explorers to claim the South Pole for Great Britain.

Sir Clements's words inspired Scott. Although he later admitted, "I have no predilection for polar exploration," Scott was determined that he would lead the Royal Society's expedition.

Robert Scott was born on June 6, 1868, in Outlands, England. Robert was the middle child in his family: he had two older sisters along with a younger brother and a younger sister. As a boy, Robert liked to daydream, although he thought of it as a bad habit. He was always small for his age and was shy and quiet.

Like many boys of that time, Robert left home at an early age. When he was 13, Robert joined the British navy as a midshipman. Midshipmen were teenage boys who joined ships and were trained to become officers. Robert spent much of his teenage years climbing in ships' rigging—the ropes hanging 120 feet over the deck of a huge naval ship.

In the navy, Robert outgrew his daydreaming habits. He became a skilled young officer. But Robert Scott wanted to be more than a sailor. He also

Nonfiction Comprehension Cliffhangers © 2008 by Tom Conklin, Scholastic Teaching Resources

wanted to experience a great adventure. So when he learned about the Antarctic expedition, he jumped at the chance to lead it.

After long months of planning, the expedition finally got under way. Back then, the only way to reach Antarctica was by boat. On August 16, 1901, Scott and his 46 men left England for New Zealand. They sailed on a ship called *Discovery*. It was specially built with heavy wood to withstand the crushing ice around Antarctica. This made the *Discovery* a very slow ship. It was late November before it finished the trip around the world to New Zealand.

Scott and his men spent a few weeks in New Zealand preparing for the trip to the South Pole. The *Discovery* set sail again on December 21, and crossed the Antarctic Circle on January 3, 1902. It slowly made its way through the ice around Antarctica. It was well into February before the *Discovery* made it to the Antarctica landmass. Since the "summer" down in Antarctica was almost over, Scott decided to hunker down and spend the winter right there.

The next months were agony. The temperatures stayed well below zero. Blizzards were harsh. Finally, when the Antarctic "spring" arrived, Scott was ready to march to the South Pole. Two separate times, Scott and two volunteers tried to reach the South Pole on foot. The distance between the *Discovery* and the pole was about 800 miles! As they made their way across the snow and ice, Scott and his men drew maps of the mountains and glaciers. They made it farther south than any people ever had—but they still failed to make it to the South Pole. In February 1904, the *Discovery* began its slow return trip to England.

Even though they had not made it to the pole, Scott and his men were greeted as heroes. Scott was eager to make a second trip to Antarctica. He was determined to be the first person to visit the South Pole, and to claim it for England.

Over the next few years, Scott fell in love with and married a woman named Kathleen Bruce. The couple had a son, whom they named Peter. Even when he was starting a family, Robert Scott never lost sight of his goal. He spent all of his time raising money and planning for a second trip to Antarctica.

On June 1, 1910, Scott set sail for Antarctica in a whaler called *Terra Nova*. (The name means "new world" in Latin.) Scott planned to use what he learned in his first journey. This time, he brought many more tools for mapping and measuring Antarctica. He also had a more careful plan for making it across Antarctica to the pole.

Just as he had in his first try, Scott would make two trips across Antarctica. But the first trip would not be an attempt to make it all the way to the South Pole. Instead, Scott and his men would set up and leave a number of camps along the way. These camps would be stocked with supplies.

Nonfiction Comprehension Cliffhangers © 2008 by Tom Conklin, Scholastic Teaching Resources

Then, on the second trip, they would have places to stay and food to eat as they fought through the bitter cold.

Unfortunately, bad weather and thick ice slowed down the *Terra Nova*. It was late in December, before the ship made it to Antarctica. Scott and his men headed across the snow to leave the supply camps for their second journey. Scott planned on leaving the biggest camp nearest the South Pole. He jokingly called this large camp "the One Ton Depot." He had carefully picked the spot for it. As he and his men traveled south, though, the weather grew impossible. Scott had to leave the One Ton Depot 20 miles north of where he had planned.

Scott and his men returned to the *Terra Nova*, where they set up camp to wait out the long, bitter Antarctic winter. Finally, on October 24, Scott left the *Terra Nova* along with 13 of his men. They began the 800-mile trek to the pole.

The journey began terribly. Just a few weeks into it, the men were trapped by a blizzard. "Our luck in weather is preposterous," Scott wrote in his diary. "The conditions are simply horrible." After five days of shivering in their tents, the men again headed off. Over the course of months, they made it from camp to camp. Finally, they neared the pole. Scott sent nine of his men back to the ship. Now Scott, along with four others, would finish the trip alone.

Scott and the others were still far from the South Pole. Tired, cold, and hungry, they trudged across the snow and ice. Still, each step brought them nearer their goal. Scott carefully kept track of their progress. After two weeks, he knew they were almost at the pole.

Early on January 16, 1912, Scott led the men on their journey south. At Scott's side was Lieutenant Henry Bowers. After a few hours of marching, Bowers stopped and yelled. Scott asked him what it was.

Bowers stared straight ahead, squinting in the glare. "I see something!" Bowers said. He pointed ahead. "There. Up ahead."

Scott stared into the distance. It took a few seconds—then he saw it, too. His heart raced, as Scott saw . . .

What do you think Robert Scott saw that January morning? Think it over, and make a prediction. Turn the page to see if your prediction was correct.

Nonfiction Comprehension Cliffhangers © 2008 by Tom Conklin, Scholastic Teaching Resources

Scott of the Antarctic

the rest of the story

Scott moaned with disappointment. There ahead, right at the South Pole, he saw a flag! Someone had beaten him to the South Pole!

As it turned out, the flag had been left there by the Norwegian explorer Roald Amundsen. Amundsen and his men had journeyed to the South Pole less than a month ahead of Scott. After all of the hardships and struggles, Scott turned out to be the second person to make it to the South Pole.

Sadly, there was worse to come. The journey back to the *Terra Nova* was a disaster. Scott and his men were caught in a blizzard miles away from the One Ton Depot. They never made it back. Another exploration party found them frozen to death in their tents a year later.

Although he did not achieve his goal, Scott is remembered as a hero in Great Britain. He is known as "Scott of the Antarctic"—a dreamer who worked and sacrificed in an effort to make his dream come true.

Nonfiction Comprehension Cliffhangers © 2008 by Tom Conklin, Scholastic Teaching Resources

On Top of the World

Curriculum Connections: Science, Social Studies, Geography

Edmund Hillary, a shy beekeeper from New Zealand, grows up determined to be the first person to climb Mount Everest.

The Cliffhanger: Edmund Hillary and his companion Tenzing Norgay make it to within 300 feet of the summit of Mount Everest, when they get caught in a blizzard. They must decide whether to risk finishing the climb or turning around to save their lives.

Answer: Hillary and Norgay persist and become the first people to reach the summit of Mount Everest.

Activating Prior Knowledge

Have students visualize how long a mile is. Then have them visualize what it would be like going a distance of almost $5\frac{1}{2}$ miles from the ground up. Tell them that's about equal to the height of Mount Everest, the tallest mountain on earth. Have them predict what sort of challenges one would face in climbing Mount Everest. Tell them they are about to read about someone who tried to climb Mount Everest.

Talk About It

☞ What is "The Death Zone"? *(The region of a mountain above 26,000 feet altitude, where the harsh weather and lack of oxygen are life-threatening.)*

☞ Why did the expedition leader let Edmund and Tenzing have one last try to make it to the summit of Mount Everest? *(Edmund argued that they had the strength to succeed.)*

Write About It

✍ Write a paragraph describing a time you overcame your fear to achieve a goal.

VOCABULARY WORDS
• • • • • • • • •

adventurer a person who enjoys taking risks

altitudes heights or distances upward

avalanche a fall or slide of a large mass of rocks and ice down a mountainside

conquer to gain a victory over

conserve to manage resources wisely

enthusiasm great excitement for or interest in something

expedition a journey or voyage made for a specific purpose

gangly awkwardly tall and skinny

imagination the ability to form mental images and make up stories

inferiority less important, valuable, or worthy

summit the highest point of a mountain

treacherous dangerous, hazardous

FOR THE TEACHER

31

On Top of the World

Young Edmund Hillary didn't look like a great adventurer. But as a boy, he did enjoy great adventures—in his imagination.

Edmund was born in Auckland, New Zealand, in 1919. His family lived in the countryside. Edmund's father, Percival, was a beekeeper who sold honey. His mother was a teacher, who made sure that her son got a good education. He traveled two hours in each direction to attend school.

Edmund was a small boy, and younger than most of his classmates. "I was a shy boy with a deep sense of inferiority that I still have," Edmund later said. He passed the four hours traveling to and from school with his nose in a book. He loved to read adventure stories. Edmund would imagine himself as the hero of the adventures that he read. "There was a phase when I was the fastest gun in the West," Edmund recalled, "then another when I explored the Antarctic." His imagination gave the small, shy boy a way to escape from loneliness.

At the age of 11, Edmund had a growth spurt. He grew 5 inches taller in one year, then 6 inches taller the next. Edmund became a gangly teenager. Although he was tall, Edmund wasn't very good at soccer or other team sports. Then, at the age of 16, Edmund took a trip that would change his life.

Every year, Edmund's school offered its students a field trip to the mountains in southern New Zealand. Edmund's father had a good year selling honey and gave his son the money to take the field trip. Edmund would never forget the experience.

The train carrying the students arrived at the Tongariro State Park at night. The moon was out and brightly lit the scenery. There was snow everywhere—in the trees, on the railroad tracks, and covering the beautiful mountains that surrounded the station. Edmund had never before seen snow. "It was really the most exciting thing to ever happen to me up to that time," Edmund said. On that trip, he learned to ski and found that he was good at it. "That was really the start of my enthusiasm for snow and ice and mountains in general," he said.

Edmund, like his father, became a beekeeper. He also did a lot of hiking in the hills outside of Auckland. From there, he tried harder climbs. He began to study mountain climbing. Edmund learned how to cut handholds in ice and rock, and how to conserve his strength in the cold and thin air at high

Nonfiction Comprehension Cliffhangers © 2008 by Tom Conklin, Scholastic Teaching Resources

altitudes. He climbed most of the mountains in the New Zealand Alps. By the time he was in his early twenties, Edmund had a new goal. He told friends that one day he would climb Mount Everest. None of his friends believed him.

Mount Everest is part of the Himalayan mountain range, and is located on the border of Nepal and Tibet. Tibetans call the mountain Chomo-Lungma, which means "mother goddess of the world." With an altitude of 29,035 feet, it's the tallest mountain in the world.

Dozens of people had tried to climb to the top of Mount Everest. None had succeeded. In 1924, the British mountain climber George Mallory had made it near the top. Other climbers in his expedition had seen him near the summit before he was lost in the snow flying in the thin air. No one ever saw Mallory alive again. In 1999, climbers found his frozen body hundreds of yards from the summit.

There are many reasons why it is so difficult and dangerous to climb a mountain like Mount Everest. The icy rocks and cliffs are treacherous. Temperatures drop far below zero. Any part of your body exposed to the air can quickly freeze. The weather can change quickly. One minute the sky could be blue, and the next minute you could be caught in a blinding blizzard. Perhaps harshest of all, the air at high altitudes is thinner than it is at sea level. Near the top of Mount Everest, there is only about one-third as much oxygen as there is at sea level. Lack of oxygen can make climbers sick and confused, leading them to make bad decisions. For all of these reasons, the area of Mount Everest higher than 26,000 feet is called "the Death Zone."

Despite the danger, Edmund Hillary was determined to conquer Mount Everest. In 1951, he made his first trip to the Himalayas. Edmund was part of an expedition there to plan a route to the top of Mount Everest. Edmund impressed everyone with his strength and ability. In the spring of 1953, he joined another expedition. This time, they weren't just studying the mountain. They were determined to climb Mount Everest. "We didn't know if it was humanly possible to reach the top," Edmund later said. "If we did get to the top, we weren't at all sure whether we wouldn't drop dead."

Edmund was one of 11 people in the group who were trying to climb Mount Everest. As they made their way up the lower part of the mountain, it was clear that one of their strongest climbers was a man they had hired to carry things. His name was Tenzing Norgay. He was a local man who had taken part in other expeditions up the mountain. As they got higher up the mountain, the climbers decided to include Tenzing in the group heading to the very top.

After days of hard climbing, the expedition made it to the southern summit of Mount Everest. They were less than 1,000 feet from the very top of

Nonfiction Comprehension Cliffhangers © 2008 by Tom Conklin, Scholastic Teaching Resources

the mountain. Two members of the expedition tried making it to the top. They got to within 300 feet, when exhaustion and bad weather forced them to stop. They returned to the others. The 12 climbers huddled together in a tent to decide what to do next. Edmund argued that he and Tenzing had the strength to succeed where everyone else had failed. The leader of the expedition, a man named John Hunt, agreed to let them try.

The next day, Edmund and Tenzing left the others and headed to the top. They slowly made their way up the icy slope. As night fell, the weather started to turn ugly. They were still well short of the top. Instead of turning back, they decided to set up camp.

Edmund and Tenzing pitched a tent on a sloping, snowy ledge more than 28,000 feet above sea level. As they sat in their thin cotton tent, they could hear the fierce wind howling outside. The weight of their bodies was the only thing that stopped the wind from blowing the tent off the mountain and onto the icy crags far below.

Sitting in their freezing tent, Edmund and Tenzing wondered what to do. Should they wait till morning, then head back to the others? If they did that, the expedition would fail.

Should they wait it out in the tent, hoping for the weather to improve? What if it only got worse?

Or should they continue on their way to the top? Could they survive another day in "the Death Zone"?

What decision did Edmund Hillary and Tenzing Norgay make? What happened next? Turn the page to find out!

Nonfiction Comprehension Cliffhangers © 2008 by Tom Conklin, Scholastic Teaching Resources

On Top of the World

the rest of the story

That night, the wind died down a little. At about 4:30 in the morning, Edmund looked out of the tent. He saw some clouds, but he also saw that the day would be clearer than the previous day. "I was absolutely certain that Tenzing and I could do this," Edmund later said. "Tenzing was keen to go. We knew that the conditions were good enough, so we just made our preparations and pushed on."

The long slope to the top of the mountain was covered with soft snow. Edmund and Tenzing moved very carefully to prevent an avalanche. At last, Edmund and Tenzing came to a ridge. They saw Tibet spread out in front of them. To their side was a small snow-capped dome. It was the summit. Edmund climbed to the top, followed by Tenzing. Together, they stood on the peak of Mount Everest.

"When we got to the top," Edmund later said, "I didn't leap around or throw my hands in the air or something. We were tired, of course, and I was very much aware of the fact that we had to get safely down the mountain again. I think my major feeling was one of satisfaction. I really did have a feeling of 'Well, we've finally made it.'"

Edmund Hillary, the shy beekeeper who dreamed of adventure, had conquered the tallest mountain in the world.

Jane of the Apes

Curriculum Connections: Science, Social Studies, Geography

Jane Goodall, a woman unable to afford college, works hard to pay for a trip to Africa. There, she meets the scientist Louis Leakey and goes on to become the world's leading authority on chimpanzee behavior.

The Cliffhanger: Alone in the wild, Jane Goodall observes two chimpanzees doing something no one has ever seen before. What?

Answer: Jane saw the chimps using tools.

Activating Prior Knowledge

Discuss with students what makes people different from animals. Focus on different behaviors—e.g., people cook food, animals do not; people travel by cars and planes, animals do not. Elicit that a major difference between animals and humans is that humans use tools all of the time, while animals do not.

Ask students to define "tool." Encourage them to be as broad as possible in their definition. Point out that simple things like pencils and toothbrushes are tools. Elicit that a tool is any object used to accomplish a task.

Talk About It

☞ What influenced young Jane to dream of exploring Africa and studying animals? (*Her pet dog Rusty, reading books like* Doctor Doolittle *and* Tarzan.*)*

☞ How did Jane get the chimps at the Gombe National Forest to trust her and act naturally when she was around? (*Jane was persistent and got the chimps to grow used to her by watching them over the course of months.*)

Write About It

✍ Imagine you are David Greybeard or Goliath. Write a first-person story describing your observations of Jane Goodall.

VOCABULARY WORDS
• • • • • • • •

accomplished completed, done

binoculars a device used to make things far away appear close at hand

emerged to come out of concealment

environmentalist a person who works to protect the air, water, plants, animals, and natural resources

habitats the areas or environments where a plant or animal lives

hurdles difficulties or problems to be overcome

similarities likenesses or resemblances

Jane of the Apes

Ever since she was a young girl growing up in England,
Jane Goodall has loved animals. When she was a year old,
her father gave her a stuffed chimpanzee doll. The doll was
Jane's favorite toy and still sits on her dresser just
as it has for more than 70 years!

Jane Goodall was born in 1934 in London, England. From her earliest days, Jane wanted to know all about animals. "Quite apart from Jubilee (the toy chimp), I have been fascinated by live animals from the time when I first learned to crawl," Jane says. For instance, when she was 5 years old, Jane and her mother were visiting Jane's grandmother in the country. Jane had been told that eggs came from hens, and she was curious to know how that happened. "I hid in a small henhouse in order to see how a hen laid an egg, and I emerged after about five hours." Jane was surprised to find that her mother had been worried sick about her. No one knew that Jane had gone to the henhouse. "My mother had even called the police to report me missing!"

When Jane was still a young girl, World War II began. She and her parents moved from the city to the country. Jane had a beloved pet dog named Rusty. Spending time with Rusty, Jane saw that animals are a lot like people. Even though they cannot talk or use tools, animals have personalities, minds, and emotions, Jane thought.

On Christmas in 1942, when she was 8 years old, Jane received the book *The Story of Doctor Dolittle* as a gift. It soon became one her favorites. The Doctor Dolittle books are fantasy stories about an animal doctor who would rather be with animals than humans. Doctor Dolittle teaches himself how to talk to animals in their own languages. Jane became fascinated with the idea of "talking" with animals.

A few years later, Jane read the Tarzan adventure novels. They are about a man who was left in the jungles of Africa as a baby and was raised by apes. The Tarzan books captured Jane's imagination. She dreamed that one day she, too, would explore Africa.

Jane graduated from high school in 1952. Although she was very bright and had been an excellent student, she did not go to college. Her family could not afford it. But Jane did not give up her dreams. She studied hard to develop her work skills, then moved to London and got a job as a secretary.

In May of 1956, an old friend of Jane's named Clo Mange wrote Jane a

Nonfiction Comprehension Cliffhangers © 2008 by Tom Conklin, Scholastic Teaching Resources

letter. Clo had moved to Kenya, in Africa, where her family owned a farm. She was writing to invite Jane to visit the family in Kenya. Jane was thrilled—visiting Africa would be her lifelong dream come true.

Jane quit her job in London and moved back to live with her mother. She got a job as a waitress and saved every penny she earned. A year later, Jane had saved enough money to buy a round-trip ticket to Africa. She left London on a ship called the *Kenya Castle* and arrived in Mombasa, Kenya, three weeks later.

Jane had a great time exploring Africa over the next few weeks. But the biggest thrill of her trip came on May 24, 1957. That's the day she met the world-famous scientist Louis Leakey.

When Jane met Dr. Leakey, he was studying the fossils found in a place called Olduvai Gorge. Leakey was exploring the oldest known remains of human beings. The fossils in Olduvai were millions of years old.

Jane joined Dr. Leakey and his wife Mary on a trip to Olduvai Gorge. There, she helped them dig up and sort fossils. Jane impressed Dr. Leakey with her intelligence and hard work. He hired Jane to become his assistant and secretary. Jane jumped at the chance.

After Jane had worked with him for a few months, Dr. Leakey made her a huge offer. He wanted to know if Jane would go to study a large group of chimpanzees living in the forests near Lake Tanganyika. Jane was overjoyed when Dr. Leakey asked if she would take on the job. After all, she had always hoped to travel to Africa and study animals. For a while, when her family could not afford to send her to college, it looked as though her dream was impossible. Now she was going to have a chance to make it come true! She left Africa and returned to England to prepare for her adventure.

There were still hurdles in the way, though. At that time, the British government controlled the country Jane wanted to live in. The people in charge would not let her live all on her own in the wilds of Africa. They insisted that someone travel with her. Jane got around this by asking her mother to make the trip with her. So in the summer of 1960, Jane and her mother arrived at the Gombe National Forest on the shore of Lake Tanganyika.

Jane's mother stayed with her for just a few months. After her mother left, Jane was alone with the chimpanzees living in the forest.

At first, the chimps were afraid of Jane and kept away from her. Jane would leave her campsite and sit near the edge of their forest home. She would watch the chimps through binoculars. After a few weeks they grew less afraid of Jane. She was able to get nearer to them, without frightening them.

Jane kept careful notes of every one of the chimps and how they

Nonfiction Comprehension Cliffhangers © 2008 by Tom Conklin, Scholastic Teaching Resources

behaved. Most scientists in her place would have identified the different chimps with numbers. Not Jane. She saw that each of the chimpanzees had a unique personality. Jane gave the animals names, not numbers.

By October of 1960, the chimps of the Gombe reservation let Jane live right among them. As she sat watching them, the chimps went about their business as if they were alone.

On November 4, Jane sat down to watch two of the chimps who lived at the reservation. She called them David Greybeard and Goliath. The two animals stood near a large mound of earth. The mound was like a giant anthill, only filled with termites instead of ants. Jane knew that the chimps often ate termites. As they stood near the mound, she wondered how the two chimps would manage to feed themselves.

What happened next astonished Jane, and would totally change the way scientists viewed apes—and human beings. As Jane watched, the two monkeys David Greybeard and Goliath . . .

What monkey business do you think Jane saw the two chimpanzees get up to? Make a prediction. Then turn the page to see if your prediction was right!

Jane of the Apes

the rest of the story

As Jane watched, the two chimps reached up to a tree and broke off twigs. After carefully pulling the leaves off the twigs, they took turns poking their twigs into the hole on top of the termite mound. As each chimp pulled his twig from the mound, it would be covered with termites—which the chimp would gobble down!

Jane gasped with awe and surprise. The two chimpanzees were using the sticks as tools. Up till then, no one had ever seen any apes—or any other animal, for that matter—make and use a tool. In fact, that was one way people defined human beings—we are the only creatures on earth to use tools. Or so we thought, until Jane Goodall went to live among the chimps.

Jane Goodall has gone on to be perhaps the world's greatest expert on chimpanzees. She is a leading environmentalist, and travels the world, educating people on nature and wildlife. But nothing she has accomplished has been more important than what she saw that November morning, as she hung out with her two friends David Greybeard and Goliath.

40

The Speckled Monster

Curriculum Connections: Health, Science, Social Studies

In a brilliant flash of insight, Dr. Edward Jenner sees that the deadly disease of smallpox can be prevented by exposing patients to a milder form of the disease.

The Cliffhanger: Dr. Jenner, having inoculated a young boy with cowpox, exposes him to smallpox germs. He waits to see if the boy comes down with the deadly disease.

Answer: Jenner's inoculation works, and the boy does not get smallpox.

Activating Prior Knowledge

Discuss with students what happens when you get sick. Make a list of things they associate with illness—medicine, doctors, staying in bed. Ask students why they stay home from school when they get a cold or flu. Elicit that others can "catch" the illness from you. Talk about how many illnesses are communicable—that is, they are passed from person to person.

Ask students if they ever have gotten a shot from a doctor. Ask if they know why young children and babies get shots. Elicit from them that children and babies are given shots to prevent them from getting diseases.

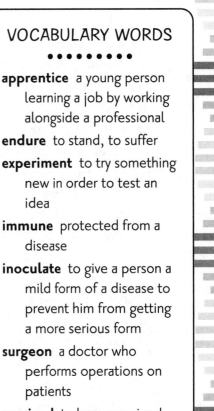

VOCABULARY WORDS
• • • • • • • • •

apprentice a young person learning a job by working alongside a professional

endure to stand, to suffer

experiment to try something new in order to test an idea

immune protected from a disease

inoculate to give a person a mild form of a disease to prevent him from getting a more serious form

surgeon a doctor who performs operations on patients

survived to have remained alive

virus a microscopic germ that causes disease

Talk About It

☞ Who first inoculated people against smallpox?
(*Chinese doctors around 1000 A.D.*)

☞ What was Edmund Jenner's brilliant idea that made inoculation safe?
(*Inoculating a patient against a mild disease can also inoculate the patient against a more serious disease.*)

Write About It

✍ Write a skit imagining how Dr. Jenner convinced James Phipps to be his guinea pig in trying out the smallpox vaccine.

The Speckled Monster

For thousands of years, a monster terrified people all across the planet. That monster was a killer disease called smallpox.

Smallpox is caused by a virus. If you breathe in the smallpox virus, about 12 days later you'll start to get sick. You will have a bad headache and backache, come down with a fever, and you will throw up constantly. A few days later, ugly pink spots will appear on your skin. Those spots will spread and grow, until your entire body is covered with hard red blisters filled with pus. If you are lucky, the blisters will eventually dry up and fall off as scabs. You will be left with bad scars for the rest of your life. If you are not lucky, you will die a slow and painful death.

For centuries, smallpox was one of the biggest killers on earth. Mummies from ancient Egypt show signs of smallpox. European explorers brought smallpox to the Americas, where it killed millions of Native Americans. It is no wonder that smallpox became known as "the speckled monster."

When you get smallpox, you have one ray of hope. If you survive the disease, you will never get it again. Once your body has fought off the disease, it is able to kill the virus if you are exposed to it again. You are immune to smallpox.

Back around 1000 A.D., doctors in China first figured out that survivors of smallpox were immune to the disease. They began to inoculate patients for smallpox. To inoculate patients, they would find someone with what seemed to be a mild case of smallpox. The doctors would take pus from the boils on the sick person's skin, and scratch it into the skin of healthy people. Those people would then get the disease. If they were lucky, the new patients would get a mild case of smallpox, and then be immune for the rest of their lives. If they were not lucky, the inoculated patients would get a full-blown case of smallpox. They would either be scarred for life or die.

By the 1700s, the idea of inoculation had made it to Europe. Smallpox was running wild in Europe in those days. Six out of ten people alive back then got the disease. Of those who got smallpox, two out of ten died. The disease was especially hard on children. Two out of every three children who died at that time were killed by smallpox.

Like many other children in the eighteenth century, a young English boy named Edward Jenner was inoculated with the smallpox virus. The experience almost killed him—and it would change the world.

Nonfiction Comprehension Cliffhangers © 2008 by Tom Conklin, Scholastic Teaching Resources

Edward Jenner was born on May 17, 1749. By the time he was 5 years old, both of his parents had died. Edward and his eight brothers and sisters were raised by his older sister, Mary.

As a boy, Edward had a great interest in nature. He collected birds' eggs and fossils. Edward was a good student, and at an early age decided that he wanted to be a doctor.

When he was still a schoolboy, Edward's family doctor decided to inoculate him with smallpox. To get him ready for the experience, the doctor wouldn't let Edward eat for days. Then the doctor exposed him to the virus. Once he was exposed, Edward was locked up with a group of other boys who had been exposed to the disease. They were left alone to get over the sickness—or die. Edward suffered badly, but he survived. He never forgot what it was like to endure smallpox. Edward vowed to save others from the illness.

When he was 14, Edward was sent to work with a surgeon. In those days, young people learned a job by being apprentices, helping adults do their jobs. After seven years as an apprentice, Edward went to London. There, he studied medicine with John Hunter, who was one of the greatest doctors of the time. Hunter taught Edward the latest in medical science. Hunter also taught Edward how to solve problems. One of Hunter's favorite sayings was "Don't think—try!" This meant that getting a bright idea wasn't enough. A true scientist must put his ideas to the test with experiments. Edward took this advice to heart.

In 1772, at the age of 23, Edward returned to the English countryside to set up shop as a doctor. His practice covered almost 400 square miles! Edward rode a horse, visiting farms and small towns, where he helped the sick. One of the biggest killers of the day was smallpox.

As a country doctor, Edward heard about many ways to treat illnesses. Many of these ways were simply "old wives' tales"—that is, legends with no basis in fact. But one old wives' tale interested Edward. Many farmers said that milkmaids—women whose job was to milk cows—never came down with smallpox. During his years as a country doctor, Edward saw that this tale was true. He never came across a milkmaid with smallpox. But why?

In May 1796, Edward got a chance to solve this mystery. That month, he saw a patient named Sarah Nelmes, who worked as a milkmaid. Sarah had a rash on her hand, and felt a little under the weather. Edward guessed that Sarah might have cowpox, a disease that affects cows. Sarah told him that one of the animals she tended, a cow named Blossom, had recently had cowpox. Sarah remembered that Blossom had had a few sores on her udder. Edward reasoned that Sarah got her rash by milking the sick cow.

As he treated Sarah, Edward had a bright idea. He knew that cowpox had things in common with smallpox: smallpox caused a horrible rash; cowpox caused a mild rash. People with smallpox got terribly sick. People with cowpox got a little bit sick. The two sicknesses were alike, with one being deadly and the other being mild. And yet, milkmaids—who were exposed to cowpox—never got smallpox. Edward's big idea:

What if cowpox was a milder form of smallpox?

If Edward's idea was true, then it would be possible to expose someone to cowpox—and that person would then be immune to the more deadly smallpox.

The more he thought about it, the more Edward was sure he had the key to defeating "the speckled monster." Edward also remembered the words of his old teacher, John Hunter: "Don't think—try!" Edward decided to test his theory.

Edward asked his gardener if he could inoculate the gardener's son, James Phipps, with cowpox. The gardener agreed. On May 14, 1796, Edward scratched James on the arm and rubbed the scratch with some pus had had taken from Sarah Nelmes's rash. Within a week, James became mildly sick with cowpox.

Next, Edward had to try the most dangerous part of his experiment. He was going to expose young James Phipps to the smallpox virus. If Edward's theory was correct, then the cowpox would have made James immune to smallpox. The disease would not affect him at all.

But if Edward was wrong, then James would get smallpox. It would make him terribly sick, and could even kill him.

On July 1, Edward Jenner exposed young James Phipps to smallpox. Then he put the boy alone in a bedroom and told everyone to stay away. Over the next few weeks, Edward kept a close watch on James . . .

Would James get sick and die? Or would Edward's idea prove to be true? What do you think happened in Edward Jennings's experiment? Turn the page to see if you're correct.

Nonfiction Comprehension Cliffhangers © 2008 by Tom Conklin, Scholastic Teaching Resources

The Speckled Monster

Edward watched James Phipps for days, and . . .

Nothing happened! James Phipps stayed healthy. Edward Jenner's idea was correct—getting a mild case of cowpox makes a person immune to the deadly killer smallpox!

Edward Jenner had come up with one of the greatest ideas in medical history—by exposing a person to a mild form of a disease, you make that person immune to deadlier forms of the disease. Edward called his idea vaccination. He got the name from the Latin word *vacca*, which means "cow."

It took time, but Jenner's idea caught on. Today, doctors vaccinate people against all sorts of diseases.

And what about smallpox? Thanks to Edward Jenner and the brave boy James Phipps, "the speckled monster" was doomed. In 1980, the World Health Organization announced that smallpox had been destroyed. For the first time in history, human beings had completely defeated a deadly disease.

Way To Go, Einstein!

Curriculum Connections: Science, Geography

Astronomers measuring the light from stars during a solar eclipse prove that Einstein's theory of relativity has upended traditional views of the universe.

The Cliffhanger: Astronomers are about to announce the results of their experiments after the eclipse of 1919, and the scientific community waits to hear whether Einstein's theory of relativity or Newton's mechanical laws of physics will be proven correct.

Answer: The results come in, and Einstein's theory of relativity is proven correct.

Activating Prior Knowledge

Brainstorm with students about the invisible forces at work in the universe, such as gravity, electricity, radio and television waves, and microwaves. Point out to students that physics is the branch of science that studies these forces and describes them with equations.

Ask students if they have ever heard of Albert Einstein. Brainstorm a list of words they associate with Einstein.

Talk About It

☞ Describe the main differences between Newton's laws and Einstein's theories. *(Newton thought space and time were constant and the universe ran like a clock. Einstein thought that space could curve and that the laws of physics are relative.)*

Write About It

✍ Write a letter to young Albert Einstein, encouraging him after his teacher told him he would never amount to anything.

VOCABULARY WORDS
• • • • • • • • •

askew out of order, disarranged

astronomers scientists studying planets, stars, and other bodies in outer space

compass a device with a needle always pointing to the North Pole

eclipse when one celestial body (the sun or moon) blocks another

gravity the force that attracts things to the earth

physics the study of physical laws at work in the universe

theoretical when something is based on a theory instead of experience

theories a set of statements devised to explain a set of facts

Way To Go, Einstein!

When Albert was 5 years old, his father gave him a gift:
a compass. It was a simple gift, but Albert was fascinated
by it. As he stared at the compass, one question
went through Albert's mind.

Why does the compass needle always point to the north? Albert was determined to find the answer. That compass pointed Albert Einstein in the direction he would take in life. Albert would try to understand the unseen forces at work in the universe.

Albert Einstein was born on March 14, 1879, in Ulm, Germany. His father, Hermann, was a scientist. His mother, Pauline, loved music. She saw to it that young Albert learned to play the violin.

When he was a boy, no one could have predicted that Albert would become a great scientist. He didn't begin to speak until he was 3 years old. And he hardly spoke at all until he was almost 10 years old. As a teenager, Albert was a poor student. He enjoyed telling jokes and sometimes disrupted his classes. He was such a bad student that one of his teachers told Albert, "Nothing will ever become of you."

Even if he did not get along with some of his teachers, Albert had a brilliant mind. He taught himself geometry and began to study physics. Physics is the study of the laws at work in nature. It uses mathematics to try to explain the "unseen forces" that had captured young Albert's imagination.

After high school, Albert left Germany to study physics at the Zurich Polytechnic in Switzerland. In 1900 he graduated and earned a teaching certificate. Still, Albert's brash personality had rubbed some of his teachers the wrong way. They would not recommend him for a teaching job. Albert finally found work. He became a clerk in the Swiss patent office. It looked as if Albert Einstein would lead a quiet, uneventful life.

Even though he did not do well in school, Albert kept up his studies. In his spare time, he worked to come up with new theories about physics. At work, he would scribble down ideas and hide them in a drawer of his desk. He later called that drawer his "department of theoretical physics." One of Albert's favorite things to do was to take long walks with his best friend. They would talk about the problems Albert was trying to solve. Albert had big ideas. He wanted to understand the entire universe.

Nonfiction Comprehension Cliffhangers © 2008 by Tom Conklin, Scholastic Teaching Resources

When Albert was young, most scientists thought the laws of the universe had already been explained by Isaac Newton. Newton was a great English scientist who had lived in the 1600s. He had written a famous study about the laws of motion in the universe. Newton's laws were based on two basic ideas about space and time. Newton thought that space is a fixed stage across which all objects in the universe move. And he thought time moves forward at the same rate for everything in the universe. According to Newton, the universe runs like a giant machine, ticking along like a clock.

Just about everyone took Newton's laws as common sense. Not Albert Einstein. To his mind, the universe was more complex. He worked hard to develop his own sets of rules to describe the laws of motion, time, and space.

The year 1905 was an amazing one for Albert Einstein. In that year, Albert, at the age of 26, published three papers on physics. Any one of them on its own would have been the work of a lifetime for any great scientist.

One of Albert's papers was on light. Scientists had debated for years whether light was made of particles—tiny bits of matter—or was instead a wave of energy. Albert proposed that light behaved as both a particle and a wave. The second of Albert's papers explained the existence of atoms and molecules.

Albert's greatest idea was in his third paper. It explained Albert's theory of relativity. According to this theory, time and space are not constant. How you experience time and space depend on where you are, and how fast you are moving compared with the speed of light. Albert's theories, if true, would totally undercut Newton's laws.

According to Newton's laws, space is rigid, like a board. To picture light moving through space, imagine a marble rolling across a board. According to Newton's laws, that marble will always roll in a straight line, even as it passes by a much larger object, such as a bowling ball.

According to Albert's theory of relativity, space is more like the surface of a trampoline than a rigid board. A large object actually bends space, as a bowling ball sitting on a trampoline bends the surface of the trampoline. If you roll a marble across the surface of a trampoline past a bowling ball, the marble's path will bend toward the larger object. In the same way, light bends toward large objects, like stars, as it passes by them—at least, according to Albert Einstein.

So, which was right—Newton's laws of a clockwork universe, or Albert's theory of relativity? It seemed like there was no way to tell for sure.

On May 29, 1919, the question would be settled. Astronomers knew that there would be a total eclipse of the sun that morning. During the eclipse, the

Nonfiction Comprehension Cliffhangers © 2008 by Tom Conklin, Scholastic Teaching Resources

light of the sun would be blocked by the moon. Astronomers would be able to measure the position of stars beyond the sun. They could then compare those measurements with ones taken when the sun was not in the sky. If the two sets of measurements were exactly the same, then the light of the stars was not affected by the sun's gravity. Newton's laws would be proven correct. If the stars appeared to be in a different position due to the sun's presence, then Albert's theory of relativity would be proven.

Astronomers picked two different locations to take their measurements from—one off the west coast of Africa, the other near Brazil. As the eclipse began the morning of May 29, they pointed their telescopes to the stars that appeared in the pale sky beyond the sun.

The astronomers took careful measurements of the stars' positions. They compared the positions of the stars near the sun with their positions in the night sky. Then they spent months studying the results. Finally, in November 1919, the astronomers called a special meeting in London. They were ready to announce the results of their experiment . . .

Which would be proved correct—Newton's laws or Albert Einstein's theory of relativity? Turn the page to see if you were right!

Way To Go, Einstein!

the rest of the story

The newspaper headlines on November 10, 1919, said it all:

"Einstein Theory Triumphs" declared the *New York Times*. "Lights All Askew in the Heavens . . . Men of science more or less agog over results of eclipse observations."

The astronomers' measurements showed that Einstein's theory of relativity was correct. His theory was a better way to describe the universe than Newton's laws. Overnight, Albert Einstein became one of the most famous people in the world.

Eventually, Einstein's theories would lead to revolutions in electronics, medicine—not to mention the invention of nuclear power.

Young Albert, the silent boy fascinated by a compass needle, had changed the world.

Nonfiction Comprehension Cliffhangers © 2008 by Tom Conklin, Scholastic Teaching Resources

The Mystery of the Messy Desk

Curriculum Connections: Health, Science, Social Studies

Researcher Alexander Fleming notices that mold spores have killed bacteria in a petri dish in his lab, leading him to discover the antibiotic medicine penicillin.

The Cliffhanger: Alexander Fleming returns from a two-week vacation to discover that something has killed bacteria samples left on his desk in his messy lab. He wracks his brain to figure out what killed the bacteria.

Answer: Fleming deduces that mold spores landed on the bacteria samples, leading him to discover penicillin.

Activating Prior Knowledge

Discuss with students the different sorts of medicines they take when they get sick. Lead the discussion so that they understand the difference between medicines such as aspirin (which are used to ease pain) and antibiotics (which help your body fight off the germs that cause sickness).

Talk About It

☞ What causes the body to get infections? *(Germs and bacteria getting into the body through cuts and other wounds.)*

☞ What is the immune system? *(The body's system for naturally fighting off infections.)*

Write About It

✍ Write a newspaper story, including a headline, describing Alexander Fleming's discovery of penicillin. Be sure to answer the five *w*'s: *who, what, when, where,* and *why.*

VOCABULARY WORDS
• • • • • • • • •

bacteria single-cell organisms that cause disease

disinfect to destroy bacteria through cleansing

fluids matter, such as liquids or gas, which flows easily

immune protected from a disease

immunology the science of how the body fights off disease

petri dish a shallow round dish used in labs

regiment a large group of soldiers in an army

serum a watery fluid

sloppiness to be untidy, messy

surgeon a doctor who performs operations on patients

The Mystery of the Messy Desk

Alexander Fleming was never a very tidy person.
Throughout his life, he kept his desk and his rooms in
a messy state. Fortunately for us, Alexander combined
a sharp mind with his sloppy habits.

Alexander Fleming was born in 1881 in Scotland. His family lived on a vast 800-acre farm miles from the nearest town. Along with his seven brothers and sisters, Alexander spent much of his time exploring the streams and hillsides of the countryside. Wandering around in nature was a huge part of Alexander's education.

By the time Alexander was 14 years old, his older brother Tom had left Scotland to become a doctor in London. Alexander was sent to London to be with his brother and go to school in the big city.

At first, Alexander studied to become a businessman. After finishing school he got a job as an office clerk. The job bored young Alex, who missed the fun he had had roaming the fields in Scotland.

When he was about 20 years old, Alexander was looking for direction in his life. His brother Tom suggested that Alexander follow in his footsteps and become a doctor.

Alexander took the tests to see if he was smart enough for medical school, and got top scores. He didn't know which of London's medical schools to go to. With no good reason to pick one school over another, he picked St. Mary's Hospital's Medical School—because he had played water polo against them and knew they had a good team!

St. Mary's Hospital had one of the world's leading researchers on germs and bacteria on its staff. That doctor, Almroth Wright, was studying how the human body fights off germs and bacteria that cause infections and disease. Although Alexander wanted to become a surgeon, he began studying with Dr. Wright. Alexander loved the mental challenge of doing research. Back then, the study of immunology—the science of how the body fights off disease—was growing quickly.

Every healthy person is born with a body that can fight off disease. Doctors call our natural ability to fight off disease our immune system. It is only when our bodies are injured, or when we are infected with powerful germs, that our immune systems fail. That's when we become sick.

Young Alexander was one of only many doctors studying the immune

Nonfiction Comprehension Cliffhangers © 2008 by Tom Conklin, Scholastic Teaching Resources

system. Those doctors discovered that certain chemicals, like iodine, can disinfect a cut or scratch. The chemicals kill the bacteria that can cause infection.

In 1914, Alexander and the rest of the world's doctors faced a huge challenge. That year, World War I broke out in Europe. Alexander joined the British army and headed to the battlefields.

The war was a giant disaster. Millions of men were mowed down by bullets and bombs. Alexander and the other doctors working to save the wounded were frustrated in their work. They found that even when they managed to treat a soldier's wounds, the soldier was still likely to die from infections.

After the war, Alexander returned to St. Mary's and his research work. He was by then a well-respected member of the school. But he still had the habits he formed as a boy in the wilds of Scotland. He was not very tidy and was also absentminded. However, his sloppiness led to his first breakthrough, in 1920.

That year, Alexander was in his lab. He held a petri dish—a round piece of glass—inside of which he was growing a sample of bacteria. Alexander felt a tickle in his nose—then he sneezed all over the petri dish. Feeling embarrassed and a little grossed out, Alexander set the dish aside and started working on another project.

Later, when he went to clean the dish, Alexander was shocked by what he saw. The dish he had sneezed on was clear of bacteria. The mucus from his sneeze had killed them. Alexander had a brainstorm. He realized that something his body had produced had killed the germs.

Alexander began working to identify the chemicals in the human body that destroy germs and bacteria. He called them "lysozymes," and found them in bodily fluids like mucus and tears.

By 1928, Alexander was studying staph infections. Staph is a nasty bacteria that can infect cuts or puncture wounds. Alexander had dozens of petri dishes loaded with staph samples lying around his messy lab. It was summer, and Alexander decided to give himself a break and take a two-week vacation.

When Alexander returned from his vacation, he decided it was time to clean up his lab. He stacked up his petri dishes and took them to sink for washing. As he scrubbed the staph cultures from the dishes, Alexander came to one dish that made him stop.

Like the other dishes, this one was covered by a film of bacteria—but with a big difference. This dish had tiny dots scattered on it. Each of the dots was surrounded by a clear "halo," where the staph infection had been killed.

Alexander's heart raced. He knew that he had stumbled onto something—but he didn't know what. Alexander retraced his steps and figured out where the dish had been left. He had stowed it on his messy desk, near an open window, before leaving for his vacation two weeks before.

So—what had happened during those two weeks? What were the tiny dots—and how had they killed the staph infection? What do you think is the solution to the mystery of the messy desk? Think it over and make a prediction. Then turn the page to discover the truth.

Nonfiction Comprehension Cliffhangers © 2008 by Tom Conklin, Scholastic Teaching Resources

The Mystery of the Messy Desk

the rest of the story

Alexander tested the tiny dots on his sample. They were a type of simple mold called penicillium. Alexander figured out that the mold spores must have drifted through the open window and landed on the dish. The weather conditions over the previous two weeks had been just right for the mold to grow. Alexander knew that something in the mold had killed the staph bacteria. He grew more of the mold and began to study it. Alexander tried to isolate the "mold juice" that had killed the germs.

It took more than ten years before doctors had a serum using the mold from Alexander's messy desk. But that serum, which Alexander named "penicillin," was a powerful antibiotic. It attacked the germs and bacteria in a body without harming the body's own immune system. In the years since, penicillin has saved millions of lives around the world. Alexander Fleming won the Nobel Prize in 1945 for his discovery of penicillin.

Years later, Alexander was visiting a modern, state-of-the-art laboratory. As he looked at the spotless lab with its sealed windows and air-conditioning, Alexander smiled. "Ah," he said, "you realize that I would never have made my discovery in these conditions. They are too clean!"

Sometimes, there's something to be said for having a messy desk.

Two Guys Named Steve

Curriculum Connections: Science, Technology

*Two misfit students, Steve Wozniak and Steve Jobs, invent the personal
computer in the Jobs family's garage.*

The Cliffhanger: Jobs and Wozniak, having
had some success selling their very first primitive
computer to other computer enthusiasts, must
come up with a name for their fledgling company.
They decide to call it . . .

Answer: Jobs and Wozniak form Apple
Computer to make and market their invention.

Activating Prior Knowledge

Brainstorm with students all of the things we use
computers for—research, communicating with
friends, playing games, writing, playing music,
watching movies, etc. Ask students what they
think the first computers were used for. Elicit that
the earliest computers were, as the name implies,
used to compute huge math problems.

Discuss with students how advances in
electronics have made computers smaller, faster,
and cheaper. Point out that decades ago, a computer as powerful as a typical
notebook computer would have easily filled a room.

> ## VOCABULARY WORDS
> • • • • • • • • •
>
> **electronics** the branch of
> science dealing with the
> flow of electrons, leading
> to the creation of
> electronic devices
>
> **engineer** a person trained in
> designing and building
> machines
>
> **fascinate** to hold an intense
> interest or attraction for
>
> **gadget** a mechanical device
>
> **industry** the people and
> companies taking part in a
> certain type of business

Talk About It

☞ How did Steve Jobs persuade Woz to start their company? *(He said that
even if they failed they'd have a good story to tell their grandkids.)*

☞ How did the first Apple computer improve on the computers that were
already being made? *(It was smaller, cheaper, and could be used with a
monitor and keyboard, making it easier to use.)*

Write About It

✍ Make an ad for the first Apple computer. Be sure to show how it is better
than other computers of the day.

Two Guys Named Steve

This is a story about two friends named Steve.

The older Steve is called "Woz" because his last name is Wozniak. He was born in 1950 in San Jose, California. Woz's dad was an engineer who worked with electronics. When he was a boy, Woz was fascinated by his dad's work. He became a nut about electronics and built his own radios. When he was 13, Woz designed and built his own calculator—and won the Bay Area Science Fair with it. Woz was a genius with electronics—and he was lonely. Naturally shy, Woz didn't have any close friends. "I was all alone," Woz later remembered.

Woz wasn't alone for long, though. When he was 18 years old, Woz met a younger boy named Steve Jobs. The two became best friends.

Steve Jobs was born in 1955 in San Francisco. He was a very bright boy but didn't do so well as a student. "I was pretty bored in school, and turned into a little terror," Steve remembers. But in fourth grade he had a great teacher named Imogene Hill. "She was one of the saints in my life," Steve recalls. "She bribed me into learning!"

Steve did so well in fourth grade that he skipped fifth grade and went straight to middle school. The middle school was very big and the kids were rowdy, and Steve was not fitting in. So his parents moved to the smaller town of Los Altos, where Steve went to Cupertino Junior High School. Steve did much better there. More importantly, Los Altos was the center of the growing electronics industry. Steve, like Woz, became fascinated with electronic gadgets.

When he got to high school, Steve heard about an older student who was an electronics whiz. That student was Woz. He and Steve met and became friends. By that time, Woz had a new passion—computers.

Back in the 1960s, computers were nothing like the ones we use today. Computers were huge machines without keyboards or screens. Computer users entered data by throwing switches on the front of the machine. Woz knew about computers because his dad used them at work. He was fascinated by them and vowed that one day he would own one himself. He told his dad about his dream. "Well, Steve," Woz's dad replied, "they cost as much as a house." That surprised Woz, who thought about it for a second. "Oh, well," Woz replied, "I'll live in an apartment."

Throughout high school, Woz spent his spare time designing computers—

Nonfiction Comprehension Cliffhangers © 2008 by Tom Conklin, Scholastic Teaching Resources

on paper. The electronics and other parts he would need to actually build the computers were far too expensive. But that didn't stop Woz from planning how a new and improved computer might work.

Steve Jobs, too, was fascinated by electronics and computers. He liked to attend after-school lectures at Hewlett-Packard, which was perhaps the world's leading electronics company. Steve was so bright and capable that he got a summer job at Hewlett-Packard, along with Woz.

After high school, Woz joined a group called the Homebrew Computer Club. It was a group of people who, like Woz, were fascinated by computers and fooled around with making their own. In the years since Woz had been in high school, engineers had invented microprocessors—also known as "computer chips." These powerful, tiny electronic circuits made it possible to design much smaller computers. Steve Jobs joined Woz at the Homebrew Computer Club.

Woz had been working on a new design for a computer that would be more powerful and much smaller than any computer around. When Steve Jobs saw the design, he knew that it was brilliant. He told Woz that they should actually build the computer. Steve argued that they could sell the computers and make some money.

Woz was not convinced. It would cost money to make the computers, and there was no guarantee that they would work or that people would want them. But Steve would not take no for an answer. He finally persuaded Woz to take the plunge. "Even if we fail," Steve said, "at least we'll be able to tell our grandkids that we started a company."

To raise the money to build their first computers, Woz sold his scientific calculator and Steve sold his VW van. Steve—a natural salesman—also talked a local electronics dealer into giving them some parts on credit. Steve and Woz then set up shop in the garage at Steve's parents' house.

Woz and Steve hired Steve's younger sister to help put the computers together. (They paid her a grand total of one dollar per computer!) After they put together the circuit boards, Woz would test them to make sure they worked. He ended up needing to repair about half the boards.

The final product was a simple computer. Unlike other, larger computers, Woz's design used a keyboard. It could also be plugged into a TV, making it the first circuit boards to use a monitor. The computer was indeed tiny—only about 8 by 11 inches. The user had to come up with a case to hold the computer. Many of theses first computers were housed in little wooden boxes!

Steve and Woz made 100 of these computers. When they were done, Woz knew that they would work. The big question was—would other computer users like them? Woz took one of the computers to his office at

Nonfiction Comprehension Cliffhangers © 2008 by Tom Conklin, Scholastic Teaching Resources

Hewlett-Packard and showed it to his co-workers. One of them fooled around with the computer for a while. He then turned to Woz with a smile on his face. "This is the most incredible product I've ever seen in my life!" he said.

Steve Jobs took the computers to the same store that had loaned him the parts. The store sold every one of them. Steve and Woz made a tidy profit off the computers. Meanwhile, Woz had ideas on how he could improve the computer. His new model would be so easy to use, Woz thought, that anyone could use it. Steve liked hearing that. He was beginning to think that computers could appeal to a whole lot of people.

On April 1, 1976, Steve and Woz started their company. But what would they call it? Steve and Woz had no trouble coming up with a name for their new company. They called it . . .

Can you guess the name of the computer company the two Steves started back in 1976? Make a prediction, then turn the page to see if your guess is correct.

Two Guys Named Steve

the rest of the story

On April 1, 1976, Steve Jobs and Steve Wozniak started Apple Computer. They picked the name because apples were Woz's favorite food. What's more, because the name starts with an A it would come at the beginning of the telephone book.

Woz's next computer—the Apple II—literally changed the world. The Apple II was the world's first personal computer that anyone could use. It was a big success and launched the personal computer industry. In the years since, personal computers have become as common as telephones and televisions.

Steve Jobs and Apple Computer went on to launch the Macintosh in 1984, which made computers even easier to use. In 2001 Apple introduced the iPod, which has become the world's most popular music player. Steve also founded the animation studio Pixar, which has made hits such as *Toy Story*, *Monsters Inc.*, *Finding Nemo*, and *Ratatouille*.

How has Woz spent the years since he invented personal computing? He has been involved in charity and has started other companies that make new electronics products. Woz has also worked at what he considers the most important job of all—he teaches fifth grade at his local public school.

Nonfiction Comprehension Cliffhangers © 2008 by Tom Conklin, Scholastic Teaching Resources

The Strange Case of the Fairy Photos

Curriculum Connections: Language Arts

Two girls cause a sensation throughout England with photographs showing themselves playing with fairies and gnomes.

The Cliffhanger:
One man, trying to determine if the fairy photos are authentic, sends them to author Arthur Conan Doyle and waits for his response. Conan Doyle writes back to say . . .

Answer:
Conan Doyle declares the photos authentic—although years later the two girls who took them admit they were fakes.

Activating Prior Knowledge

Discuss with students how easy it is to fake photos with digital cameras and software like Photoshop. Point out to students that before digital technology it was much, much harder to fake a photo. To many people back then, a photograph was as real as something you see with your own eyes.

Lead a conversation on mythical creatures, such as ghosts, elves, and giants. Ask students if they think any of these mythical creatures might actually exist.

Talk About It

☞ How do you think that Frances and Elsie were able to make the fake photos that fooled so many people? *(Elsie was a good artist and worked at a photo-lab, so she understood how cameras work.)*

Write About It

✐ Pretend you are Sir Arthur Conan Doyle. Write a persuasive essay to reply to people who think that the photos Elsie and Frances made were fakes.

VOCABULARY WORDS
• • • • • • • • • •

exposure in photography, the moment a photo is taken

fluttering a motion made by flapping up and down

gnome a small mythical creature resembling an old man

improbable unlikely

insisted to assert something firmly

lecturer an expert giving a talk on a subject

mischievous playfully annoying

reluctantly with hesitation

scoured searched thoroughly

skeptical showing doubt

The Strange Case of the Fairy Photos

Frances Griffiths was bored.

Frances, only 9 years old, was staying with her mother at her cousin's house in Cottingley, England. The year was 1917, and World War I had been raging for years. Before the war, Frances and her mother had been living in South Africa.

Cottingley was very different from South Africa. The weather in England was cool and wet. The house in Cottingley was surrounded by trees. A beautiful stream, with a small waterfall, ran in the woods near the house. Frances spent many hours exploring the woods and lying on the mossy banks of the stream, daydreaming.

Frances often spent time with her cousin, Elsie. Elsie was 16 years old and was a good artist. For three years, she had worked at a part-time job in a photo lab, hand-tinting black-and-white photos. When she wasn't working or going to school, Frances passed the time with her young cousin.

One sunny day in July 1917, Frances and Elsie came home after spending the day at the stream. Frances's mother took one look at the young girl and angrily asked what had happened. Frances's shoes and dress were soaking wet. Frances, thinking fast, said that she had fallen into the stream while she had been playing with the fairies who lived in the woods near the water.

Frances's mother could hardly believe her ears. Her daughter had been playing with fairies? It was *their* fault that she had almost ruined her shoes? This was the worst excuse she had ever heard. As punishment, her mother sent Frances up to her room.

Elsie felt sorry for her cousin and went up to the bedroom with Frances to share her punishment. Later that night, the two girls came down from the room. By this time, Elsie's father had heard the story about Frances and the fairies. He called the two girls into his study, where he asked them if they wanted to take back the wild tale.

The girls did not take back the story. They insisted that they had both spent many happy hours playing with the fairies who lived near the stream. Not only that, they said that they could prove that they were telling the truth. If Elsie's father would let them use his camera, they would take photographs of the fairies who lived in the woods near the stream.

Nonfiction Comprehension Cliffhangers © 2008 by Tom Conklin, Scholastic Teaching Resources

And so began one of the strangest stories of the past 100 years.

The next sunny day, Elsie's father loaded the camera with film and gave it to the two girls. They headed off to the woods to find their fairy playmates. A few hours later, they returned with the camera. The girls gave the camera to Elsie's father, who headed off to his darkroom to develop the photos they had taken. The girls went along with him.

There was only one picture in the camera. As Elsie's father began to develop it, he saw that it was a close-up of his young niece. As the photo became more clear, he noticed something blurry in the foreground near Frances's face. He asked what the blurry image was—the paper they had wrapped their sandwiches in? No, the girls replied, it was their playmates from the woods. As the photo grew more clear, Elsie's father saw the image showed tiny people with see-through wings. They were dancing fairies! More irked than awed, he gave the girls their photo and said that it didn't prove anything.

The girls did not back down from their story. Each night, their parents would ask them to tell the truth about the fairies in the woods. They wanted the girls to admit they had faked the photographs. But the girls insisted that there were fairies in the woods.

One month later, Elsie and Frances asked Elsie's father if they could borrow his camera again. He reluctantly agreed. The girls came back later in the day and said they had another photo. Elsie's father developed it. The picture showed Frances sitting in the grass with a big smile on her face. Next to her, dancing a little jig, was a mischievous-looking gnome.

There, the girls said. Doesn't that prove it? Now they had two photos showing the fairies who lived in the woods. Elsie's father had one thing to say to that: the girls had borrowed his camera for the last time!

The adults in the house were determined to get to the bottom of the story. They searched the girls' room for evidence that they had faked the photos. They also scoured the woods and stream, looking for clues. They didn't find anything—no cutouts of the fairies that had appeared in the photos, no little dolls—nothing. The girls' fathers were certain that the girls had played a trick and had somehow faked the pictures.

Elsie's and Frances's mothers, though, were not quite so sure. The two women took part in the spiritualism movement, which was popular in England at that time. Spiritualists believe in ghosts. Their mothers knew that Elsie and Frances probably had played a trick on them. But they also thought that maybe, just maybe, the girls had seen fairies out in the woods.

Two years later, Frances's mother was attending a meeting of spiritualists. The topic was "fairy life." The lecturer claimed that fairies and gnomes actually exist. After the meeting, Frances's mother told other people in the meeting about the photos her daughter and niece had taken. The lecturer asked to see the photos. Frances's mother sent him the photos—and he was amazed by them. Convinced that they were real, the lecturer sent the photos to Edward Gardner, one of the leaders of the spiritualism movement in England.

Gardner saw the photos and thought that they might be real. He shared them with a friend of his, Harold Snelling, who was an expert in photography. What Snelling had to say excited Gardner:

"These dancing figures are not made of paper nor of any fabric; they are not painted on a photographed background—but what gets me most is that all these figures have moved during exposure."

According to Snelling, the photos showed actual, true-life fairies!

Gardner visited the girls in Cottingley and had them show him where the fairies lived. The girls told him that the fairies were shy and would only come out for the girls. Gardner left the girls a camera and begged them to take more pictures. The girls were happy to do so. Two weeks later, they mailed Gardner two more photos. One showed Elsie with a fairy fluttering in front of her face. The other was a blurry shot of fairies dancing in a circle.

Gardner was now convinced that the photos were genuine. But he decided to get one last opinion before making the photos public. He sent the photos to one of the most famous men in England—the writer Arthur Conan Doyle.

Arthur Conan Doyle was best known for creating the character Sherlock Holmes. Sherlock Holmes was the world's greatest detective. He was cold and logical, and used science to solve crimes. Conan Doyle summed up Sherlock Holmes's philosophy in one famous sentence: "When you have eliminated the impossible, whatever remains, however improbable, must be the truth." If anyone would look at the photos with a skeptical eye, it would be the man who had invented Sherlock Holmes.

Arthur Conan Doyle was visiting Australia at the time. Gardner sent him the photos, along with a letter explaining the story, and asked for his opinion on the matter. Weeks later, Gardner got a letter from Australia. It was from Conan Doyle. Gardner nervously opened the envelope, eager to see what the great author thought of the photos . . .

What did Arthur Conan Doyle make of the strange case of the fairy photos? And what happened next? Predict what you think happened. Then turn the page to see what really happened.

Nonfiction Comprehension Cliffhangers © 2008 by Tom Conklin, Scholastic Teaching Resources

The Strange Case of the Fairy Photos

the rest of the story

Arthur Conan Doyle had spent many hours studying the photos. He was certain of one thing:

The photos were not fakes. Elsie and Frances had photographed real live fairies! After all, Conan Doyle thought, how could two girls have cooked up a hoax like this?

Not only was Conan Doyle convinced that the photos were real, he also published them in the magazine the *Strand*, which also published his Sherlock Holmes stories. A few years later, he wrote a book, *The Coming of the Fairies*, which made Frances and Elsie famous.

People were torn by the story. A few people agreed with Conan Doyle. Most people, though, thought he had lost his mind. The photos were obvious fakes, they said. For their part, Elsie and Frances stayed mum.

Finally, in 1983, when they were both old ladies, Elsie and Frances told the truth. The fairies were drawings Elsie had made. The girls had used pins to make it look as if the fake fairies were standing, dancing, and flying. The whole thing had been a hoax.

But even though the photos were fake, Frances insisted, she really had seen fairies back by the stream in Cottingley.

Mars Attacks!

Curriculum Connections: Language Arts, Media Studies

Millions of people across the country panic at hearing a radio broadcast of "The War of the Worlds" the day before Halloween in 1938.

The Cliffhanger: A panicked New Yorker, convinced by a radio broadcast that Martians are attacking his city, gets into a cab and hears a shocking announcement on the radio. What does he hear?

Answer: The announcer—director, writer, performer Orson Welles—tells his audience that the broadcast has been a Halloween trick.

Activating Prior Knowledge

Discuss with students how they get the news. Talk about how many people learn about what is going on in the world by watching television and listening to the radio. Ask students if they were ever watching a program that was interrupted by a breaking news story. Elicit that broadcasters will only interrupt their programming for very important news.

Point out to students that radio used to be the only broadcast medium. Talk about what it would be like in a world with no television or Internet—only radio. Point out that radio used to have more than just music, news, and talk shows. In the past, many radio shows presented plays and dramas.

VOCABULARY WORDS
• • • • • • • • •

cinders ashes

cylinder a solid shape with a round base and top, like a can

establishment a business, such as a restaurant

glistens has a wet, sparkling shine

hoax a trick

luminous giving off light

Martians fictional creatures from the planet Mars

meteorite a stone that has fallen to earth from outer space

trampled to have been beaten down by feet

Talk About It

☞ Why do you think Orson Welles decided to broadcast "The War of the Worlds" at the end of October? *(It was a Halloween prank.)*

Write About It

✍ Imagine you were one of the people who were fooled by the broadcast. Write a letter to a radio station that aired it, expressing your views on the show.

Mars Attacks!

Believe it or not, the following is a true story. It all began
shortly after 8 p.m. on Sunday, October 30, 1938 . . .

Louis Winkler was sitting in his living room in New York, listening to the
radio. This was in the days before television, and people relied on the radio
for news and entertainment. Winkler had his radio tuned to one of the most
popular shows of the day. About 12 minutes into the show, a comedy act
ended and the program began playing classical music. Winkler, along with
millions of other listeners, decided to see what was on the other stations.

Winkler tuned in to WABC. That station was playing some easy-listening
dance music. Winkler settled back and relaxed, enjoying the music.

Suddenly, an announcer broke in on the tunes.

"Ladies and gentlemen, here is the latest news bulletin from the
Intercontinental Radio News. It is reported that a huge, flaming object,
believed to be a meteorite, fell on a farm in the neighborhood of Grovers Mill,
New Jersey."

Louis Winkler sat up, interested. New Jersey was just across the river
from where he lived.

Meanwhile, Emanuel Priola was working in West Orange, New Jersey. It
was a quiet night at the establishment, with only six customers. Priola tuned
the radio to WABC. What he heard shocked him. A news reporter was on the
scene where the "meteorite" had crashed, about 40 miles away.

"Well, I hardly know where to begin, how to paint a word picture of the
strange scene before my eyes," the reporter said. Emanuel and his customers
grew quiet and listened to the radio. "The object doesn't look very much like a
meteor. It looks more like a huge cylinder . . . Just a minute! Something's
happening! The end of the thing is beginning to flake off! The top is beginning
to rotate like a screw! The thing must be hollow! Stand back! Ladies and
gentlemen, this is the most terrifying thing I have ever witnessed."

By now, Emanuel and his customers were beginning to panic.

"Wait a minute!" The newscaster was shouting now. "Someone is crawling
out of the hollow top. Someone or . . . something. I can see peering out of
that black hole two luminous disks . . . are they eyes? It might be a face . . .
I can see the thing's body now. It's large, large as a bear, and it glistens like
wet leather. But that face . . . I can hardly force myself to keep looking at it,
it's so awful. The eyes are black and gleam like a serpent's."

Emanuel Priola had heard enough. He told his customers that he was closing. Emanuel told them all to do what he was going to do—go home and protect his family from the weird creatures who had landed in Grovers Mill.

In Brooklyn, New York, the police were flooded with calls. In just a matter of minutes, more than 800 people called the station. Most of them were in a panic over the radio report of strange creatures landing in New Jersey.

At about 8:30, Samuel Tishman came home from a stroll on the Upper West Side of Manhattan. His phone began to ring. The caller was his nephew, who was in a panic. New York City was about to be attacked, Tishman's nephew said. By who? Tishman asked. Creatures from outer space, his nephew said. At first, Tishman thought his nephew was playing a joke. His nephew told Tishman to turn on the radio.

"Ladies and gentlemen, I have a grave announcement to make," the radio announcer began. "Incredible as it may seem . . . those strange beings who landed in the Jersey farmlands tonight are part of an invading army from the planet Mars."

Tishman gulped. He knew that his nephew had not been joking.

"U.S. Armed Forces battled the creatures moments ago," the radio announcer went on. "The battle which took place has ended in one of the most startling defeats ever suffered by an army. Seven thousand men armed with rifles and machine guns pitted against a single Martian fighting machine. There were one hundred and twenty survivors. The rest are strewn over the battlefield, crushed and trampled to death under the metal feet of the monster, or burned to cinders by its heat ray."

Tishman grabbed some clothes and rushed from his apartment. If the monsters were in New Jersey, then they'd be in New York any minute. That meant he had to leave—and now!

Tishman made it to the street outside of his apartment building. Hundreds of terrified people were already in the street, suitcases in hand, ready to flee the Martians.

Across the Hudson River in Newark, New Jersey, the police received thousands of calls. Not all of the callers were terrified people asking how to escape from the Martians. Hundred of doctors and nurses called to volunteer to help care for the people injured by the Martian attackers. City officials also called in, with plans to set up emergency aid for the city's population.

All across the United States, people listened with terror to the radio reports of the Martian attack.

Newspapers in Chicago were swamped with calls. Many of the callers had relatives in New Jersey, and they wanted to know if lists of the people killed there were available.

Nonfiction Comprehension Cliffhangers © 2008 by Tom Conklin, Scholastic Teaching Resources

In Indianapolis, a woman ran into a church in the middle of its weekly service. "New York is destroyed!" she screamed. "It's the end of the world. You might as well go home to die. I heard it on the radio." The service ended as everyone left the church in a panic.

In Pittsburgh, a man found his wife in the bathroom holding a bottle of poison. In the next room, the radio was blaring. A news announcer was telling how Martians had sent a cloud of poison gas over New York City. "I'd rather die this way than like that," the man's wife sobbed.

Meanwhile, in New York City, Samuel Tishman made his way to Broadway. He needed to find a way out of the city. Tishman hailed a cab, which pulled over. Tishman told the cab driver they had to leave the city. The cab driver, who had been listening to music on the radio, was surprised and asked why. Tishman told him about the Martian attack. The driver didn't believe him, so Tishman told him to change stations. The driver did so.

The cab's radio tuned in to WABC, the station Tishman had been listening to. Tishman heard a radio announcer's voice. What the announcer said shocked Tishman. In fact, it took a moment for Tishman to believe his ears . . .

What do you think happened next? After reports of Martian landings and giant monsters armed with "heat rays" and poison gas, what could the announcer have said to shock the listeners even more? Turn the page to find out.

Nonfiction Comprehension Cliffhangers © 2008 by Tom Conklin, Scholastic Teaching Resources

Mars Attacks!

the rest of the story

"This is Orson Welles," the announcer said, "this broadcast of 'The War of the Worlds' is simply our radio version of dressing up in a sheet and jumping out of a bush and saying 'boo!'"

The entire thing had been a hoax! The writer and director Orson Welles had come up with a radio version of the classic science fiction story "The War of the Worlds." But he and the other actors had performed the story as if it were really happening. The show was meant as a Halloween joke.

But Samuel Tishman, Louis Winkler, and millions of other terrified listeners were not laughing.

"I almost had a heart attack!" Winkler told the *New York Times*. "In my mind it was a pretty crummy thing to do."

What do you think?

Nonfiction Comprehension Cliffhangers © 2008 by Tom Conklin, Scholastic Teaching Resources

The Greatest Fish Story Ever Told

Curriculum Connections: Science, Social Studies

*A young museum curator in South Africa finds the body of a coelacanth (**see**-la-canth)—a fish thought to have been extinct for 65 million years— among the catch on a local fishing boat.*

The Cliffhanger: Weeks after finding a weird fish on a local fishing boat, museum curator Marjorie Courtenay-Latimer finally gets a response to the desperate letters she sent to a local fish expert. Having seen her description of the strange fish, the expert says—what?

Answer: Courtenay-Latimer had uncovered a specimen of a coelacanth—a fish that was supposed to have gone extinct with the dinosaurs.

Accessing Prior Knowledge

Discuss dinosaurs with students. Talk about how dinosaurs went extinct 65 million years ago. Then discuss what kind of sensation would be caused if someone, somewhere, found an actual living, breathing dinosaur somewhere in the world. Then have the students read the story.

Talk About It

☞ Why did Captain Goosen have Marjorie come down to the docks? *(He knew she would be interested in the strange fish they had caught.)*

☞ Why did Dr. Smith not return Marjorie's calls and first letters about the fish? *(He had been away on vacation.)*

Write About It

✍ Imagine some hunters find a live dinosaur in a rain forest. Write a story about the discovery and what happens after.

VOCABULARY WORDS
• • • • • • • • •

curator the person in charge of a museum's collections and exhibits

endangered threatened

extinct no longer in existence

resembles looks like

specimen an example regarded as typical of its class

taxidermist a craftsman who stuffs the skins of animals for display

telegram a message sent by telegraph

viciously with anger, mean

volunteer to perform a service without being paid

The Greatest Fish Story Ever Told

Fishermen are famous for telling tall tales. No matter how many
fish a fisherman will catch, the best fish is always the one
that got away. Well, this story is about the most incredible fish
ever caught—and how it almost "got away."

It all began on December 22, 1938, in East London, South Africa. East London
is a city on the coast of the Indian Ocean. It is home to a small natural
history museum. Back in 1938, the museum's curator—the person in charge
of the exhibitions—was a young woman named Marjorie Courtenay-Latimer.

That December day, Marjorie was busy in the museum. She was
preparing an exhibition on reptiles. On top of that, she was planning for
Christmas, which was only three days away.

As Marjorie worked, her phone rang. On the other end was the manager
of a local fleet of fishing boats. Marjorie was friends with Hendrik Goosen, the
captain of a fishing boat called the *Nerine*. The fleet manager was calling to
let Marjorie know that Captain Goosen had come back from a fishing trip—
and that he had caught a very strange fish.

Marjorie hesitated. After all, she had a lot of things to do before
Christmas. Still, Marjorie decided to make the trip down to the dock. She
liked Captain Goosen, and at the very least would wish him and his crew a
merry Christmas. Marjorie and her assistant got into a taxi and headed down
to the docks.

When they got there, Marjorie headed to the *Nerine*. The boat was a
trawler, which meant that it dragged a huge net behind it, catching tons of
fish in the net as it moved through the water.

Marjorie wished Captain Goosen and his crew a merry Christmas.
Goosen told her that she should look through their catch—the crew had
brought in a strange fish. Marjorie glanced at the huge pile of dead fish lying
on the deck of the boat. She did not exactly feel like sorting through them all.
Marjorie was about to leave the boat and head back to the museum, when
something caught her eye.

Marjorie had seen a large blue fin poking out of the pile of dead sharks
and rays. She reached down and tugged on the fish it belonged to. Marjorie
managed to yank it out from under the pile of fish—and gasped at what
she saw.

The mystery fish was almost 5 feet long, and was silvery blue in color. It
had a large, square head, with dead eyes and rows of sharp teeth. Its tail had

Nonfiction Comprehension Cliffhangers © 2008 by Tom Conklin, Scholastic Teaching Resources

an odd, three-part shape. Strangest of all, the fish had four fins along its underside. To Marjorie, the fins looked like stubby legs!

As Marjorie stared at the weird fish, one the boat's crew came to her side. He shook his head at the fish and told Marjorie that he'd been a fisherman for 30 years and had never seen anything like it before.

Marjorie asked if the fish had been alive when they caught it. Oh, yes, the crew told her. In fact, the fish had snapped viciously at them as it flopped around on the deck. It lived for quite a long time even after it had been caught.

Marjorie tingled with excitement. She didn't know what exactly the men of the *Nerine* had caught, but she knew that she had to get it back to the museum. Marjorie asked Captain Goosen if she could have the fish. He smiled and told her that's why he'd called her. Marjorie asked if they had something she could wrap the fish in. The fishermen searched the boat and the dock, and someone found a large sack. Marjorie wrapped the fish in the sack and, with her assistant's help, lugged the 127-pound beast back to the taxi they had brought from the museum.

By this time, the mystery fish was starting to smell pretty bad. The taxi driver saw Marjorie and her assistant hauling the large sack and asked what they had in it.

"A specimen for the museum," Marjorie replied. The taxi driver leaned over and sniffed the bag. He shook his head—there was no way they were going to get into his cab, not with that smelly thing. Marjorie begged and pleaded, then got very angry. At last, the taxi driver agreed to take them to the museum.

Back at the museum, Marjorie made a phone call to her friend Professor J. L. B. Smith. He taught chemistry at a college a few miles away. He was also an amateur ichthyologist—that is, a scientist who studies fish. Unfortunately, Smith was not in his office that day.

Marjorie hung up the phone and looked at the weird fish. It is summertime in December down in South Africa, so the weather was warm. And the big dead fish wasn't smelling any better! Marjorie called up Robert Center, who was the taxidermist she always used to prepare animals for display in the museum.

Center showed up at the museum to prepare the fish. He carefully cut open the fish and removed its guts and gills. The skin, scales, and skeleton of the fish would be stuffed and preserved. As he began work on the fish, the taxidermist noticed some strange things about it. For one thing, each of the fish's large scales was filled with a thick oil. As he cut open the fish, Center saw that it had no skeleton. The fish did have a backbone, however. The backbone was about an inch thick. As Center stuck the point of his knife into the backbone, oil spurted out of it!

The next day Marjorie tried calling J. L. B. Smith a second time. Again, he was not in his office. Since she couldn't get him on the phone, Marjorie decided to write him a letter.

First, Marjorie sat down and made a detailed sketch of the fish, pointing out all of its most interesting parts. She then fed some paper into her typewriter and began to write:

Dear Dr. Smith,
I had the most queer-looking specimen brought to notice yesterday . . .

Marjorie then went on to describe the fish and how it had been caught. When she had finished the letter, Marjorie put it and her sketch into an envelope and mailed them to Smith.

The next few days were difficult. Marjorie hardly enjoyed her Christmas, as she waited nervously for Smith to get back to her. "I couldn't think about anything but the fish," Marjorie later recalled. "I checked the post every day and waited for a phone call, but there was no word from Smith."

The day after Christmas, Marjorie heard complaints at the museum. She had saved the mystery fish's guts and gills—but they were smelling so bad that people were getting sick. Marjorie reluctantly let her assistant toss the guts and gills into the garbage.

As New Year's came and went, Marjorie began to have second thoughts. It had been more than a week since she had written to Smith, and he had not bothered to respond. He was the fish expert, after all. Maybe she had been wrong. Maybe the fish was nothing special.

Finally, on January 3, Marjorie received a telegram at the museum. It was from Smith, and it was one sentence long:

MOST IMPORTANT PRESERVE SKELETON AND GILLS (OF) FISH DESCRIBED

Marjorie's heart raced. She had been right—the fish must be some great discovery! But she had already gotten rid of its gills and guts. Marjorie got on the phone to see if the garbage had been taken to a dump. She was ready to pick through the trash herself to find the guts and gills. Alas, she was told that the town's garbage was dumped at sea.

The next day, Marjorie finally got a letter from Smith. In it, he explained that he'd been away on vacation and had only received her letter after New Year's Day. He had mailed the letter, then sent her the telegram so that she would know to preserve as much of the fish as possible.

Marjorie's pulse raced with excitement as she read the next sentence.

What weird creature did the fisherman catch that day in 1938? Make your prediction—then turn the page to see if you were correct.

Nonfiction Comprehension Cliffhangers © 2008 by Tom Conklin, Scholastic Teaching Resources

The Greatest Fish Story Ever Told

the rest of the story

Dr. Smith had written in his letter:

From your drawing and description the fish resembles forms which have been extinct for many a long year . . .

In fact, the fisherman had caught a living coelacanth (pronounced **see**-la-canth). The oldest fossil of a coelacanth is 360 million years old. The "youngest" coelacanth fossils are 65 million years old. Scientists had thought that the coelacanth died out with the dinosaurs. Marjorie Courtenay-Latimer had "caught" a fish that everyone thought had been extinct for millions of years!

In the years since, scientists have found other coelacanths living in different parts of the Indian Ocean. Although they are endangered, the oldest known fish still swim the seas.

Who knows what other mysteries swim in the deep, dark oceans?

"The Play"

Curriculum Connections: Social Studies, Physical Education

The University of California, Berkeley, Golden Bears beat their fierce rivals, the Stanford University Cardinals, by returning a kickoff for a touchdown after time has expired. The play features five lateral passes . . . and the Stanford marching band!

The Cliffhanger:
After the Cal Bears appear to have run back a kickoff for a touchdown with no time left on the clock, the game's referees huddle to determine if the play counts. Tens of thousands of fans watch as the head ref turns to signal . . .

Answer:
Touchdown! The play counted, and Cal won one of the wildest football games ever played.

VOCABULARY WORDS
• • • • • • • • •

bitter unpleasant

managed to somehow bring
about

rivalries competitions that
span time

Activating Prior Knowledge

Lead a discussion about sports rivalries. Use a rivalry from local teams as a framework for the discussion. Discuss how fans of the rival teams remember games for years, and like to relive the most exciting moments from the rivalry.

Have a football fan describe the rules regarding lateral passes and forward passes. (Basically, once the football has passed the line of scrimmage it is against the rules to throw a forward pass. However, it is possible to throw the ball from side to side or backward.)

Talk About It

☞ Why was the 1982 game between Cal and Stanford so important to Stanford? *(Because Stanford hoped to go to a bowl game and earn the Heisman Trophy for their star player, John Elway.)*

☞ Why did Stanford kick off from the 25-yard line at the end of the game? *(Because they had been penalized 15 yards for celebrating too much after scoring the go-ahead field goal.)*

Write About It

✍ What's the most exciting sports play you ever saw? Write a paragraph to describe it. Be sure to describe where and when it happened and why it was so exciting.

"The Play"

There are many great rivalries in sports. One of the
most bitter rivalries in college football is between
Stanford University and the University of California.

The Cardinals of Stanford have played Cal's Golden Bears every year since
1897. The winning team takes home a trophy called the Stanford Axe. The
two teams battle fiercely to win the trophy, which the winning school displays
until the next year's game.

In 1982, the big game between Stanford and Cal was even bigger than
usual. Cal had won six games and lost four that year, and the game against
Stanford would be the last one of their season. Stanford, on the other hand,
had high hopes. Stanford's star player was quarterback John Elway. He
was one of the top players in the country, but had never led his team to a
bowl game. With a win against Cal, there was a good chance that his team
would finally play in a bowl. Elway could also win the Heisman Trophy,
which is given to the player chosen as the best college player of the year.
There was a lot on the line for Stanford as they squared off against Cal on
November 20, 1982.

A sellout crowd cheered as the two teams took to the field at California
Memorial Stadium. The stadium was Cal's home field, and most of the fans
were there to root for the Golden Bears. Still, Stanford was just a few miles
away. Many Stanford fans were in the stands, too. The Stanford band,
famous for its lively half-time and postgame shows, took up most of the seats
behind one end zone.

The game started as a tough defensive struggle. After a scoreless first
quarter, Cal took the lead with a field goal in the middle of the second
quarter. A few minutes later, Cal scored again with a touchdown pass. At
halftime, Cal took a 10–0 lead into the locker room.

John Elway came out in the second half ready to prove that he was the
best player going. He led the Cardinals on two long drives, both ending with
touchdown passes. The Cardinals were ahead, 14–10. But Cal scored the next
nine points to take a 19–14 lead. Late in the fourth quarter, Stanford kicked a
field goal, making the score 19–17. Then Elway and the Cardinals got the ball
back with a minute left to play and one last chance to win the game.

Elway's first toss was a screen pass to running back Vincent White.
White slipped and fell after catching the ball, losing seven yards. Elway's
second pass fell incomplete. That made it third down, with 17 yards to go.

Elway dropped back to pass again—the throw was batted away by a Cal defender.

It was fourth down and 17. The ball was on the 13-yard line with less than a minute to play. Elway had one last chance to save the game. He dropped back to pass, looked down the field, and zipped a perfect pass 29 yards down the field—the receiver caught it! Stanford had a first down near midfield!

On the next play, John Elway dropped back to pass again—and again, he found an open receiver! This pass was good for another 20 yards. Stanford was getting close to field-goal range. On the next play, Elway and the Cardinals crossed up the Cal defense by running the ball. The running back darted outside for another 20-yard gain. Now Stanford had the ball inside Cal's 20-yard line, with only 20 seconds left to play. Stanford's fans were screaming with joy as Elway led his team down the field in this amazing comeback.

After one more run for no gain, Elway called time-out. There were only eight seconds left on the clock as the Stanford kicker, Mark Harmon, trotted onto the field. The two teams lined up—the ball was snapped—and Harmon kicked the ball up and through the uprights. The kick was good! Stanford took the lead, 20–19!

The Stanford team mobbed kicker Harmon as the Stanford marching band streamed from the stands to start its postgame celebration. In the press box, radio announcer Joe Starkey told his listeners that Stanford's comeback had made this one of the greatest football games ever.

But the Stanford team was celebrating a bit too early. There were still four seconds left on the clock, and that was time enough for a kickoff. The officials pushed the celebrating Stanford players to the sidelines. In the far end zone, the Stanford band was herded off the field, ready to start playing once the game was over. "Only a miracle can save the Bears!" radio announcer Joe Starkey said.

The kicking team lined up on its own 25-yard line, since Stanford had been penalized 15 yards for its celebration. Cal's receiving team took the field, confused and discouraged. In fact, they were so disorganized that only ten players were on the field for Cal. Mark Harmon, who had just kicked the field goal for Stanford, trotted to the ball and made a "squib" kick. The ball bounced about 40 yards down the field . . . and then the craziness began.

Kevin Moen of the Bears picked up the ball and ran upfield. He made it only a few yards, when he was swarmed by Stanford defenders.

Moen stopped and tossed the football all of the way across the field to Richard Rodgers. Rodgers darted down the sideline. A bunch of Stanford

Nonfiction Comprehension Cliffhangers © 2008 by Tom Conklin, Scholastic Teaching Resources

defenders blocked his way, so Rodgers flipped the ball back to Dwight Garner.

Garner, surrounded by Stanford players, put his shoulders down and plowed ahead. Four Stanford defenders grabbed Garner and began to drag him down. He was a split second from being tackled, when Garner managed to chuck the football out of the pile and back into the hands of his teammate Richard Rodgers.

As Garner disappeared in the pile of Stanford players, it looked as if he had been tackled and the game was over. The Stanford band, thinking their team had won the game, began to pour onto the field to play.

Meanwhile, Rodgers took the ball and rushed the field. As Stanford players approached, Rodgers tossed the ball back to his teammate Mariet Ford. Ford caught the ball in stride and raced down the field—past the 30, the 20—as he neared the end zone, Ford was ganged up on by four Stanford players. They grabbed Ford, ready to tackle him. Ford, without looking, flipped the ball into the air . . .

And into the arms of his teammate Kevin Moen! Moen darted down the field, dodging fans and members of the Stanford band who had already strutted onto the grass. Moen dashed across the goal line untouched—where he promptly plowed into trombone player Gary Tyrell of the Stanford band.

There was utter chaos on the field. The Stanford fans and team could not believe that Cal had run the kickoff back for a touchdown.

"Will it count?" asked radio announcer Joe Starkey, as the referees huddled to talk over the play. "There are penalty flags all over the place. Wait and see what happens—we don't know who won the game."

The fans and players held their breath as the referees talked over the play. Finally, the head referee turned away from the others. They had reached a decision.

The referee signaled . . .

What do you think happened next? Make a prediction, then turn the page to see of you were correct.

"The Play"

the rest of the story

Touchdown!

The referees decided that Cal had scored a touchdown on the kickoff. The penalty flags were because Stanford had too many men on the field. And even if Kevin Moen had not made it to the end zone, Cal still would have been awarded a touchdown because Stanford's band had interfered with the play.

The game's final score: Cal 25, Stanford 20.

The stadium went crazy. Up in the press box, radio announcer Joe Starkey was yelling into his microphone. "The Bears have won! The Bears have won the most amazing, sensational, dramatic, heartrending, exciting, thrilling finish in the history of college football! California has won the Big Game over Stanford!"

For John Elway, there would be no bowl game that year, and no Heisman Trophy. Fortunately for him, he would go on to have a great NFL career, including MVP awards and Super Bowl wins.

For Stanford band member Gary Tyrell, who had been run over in the end zone, the game left nothing but bitter memories and a dented trombone.

Nonfiction Comprehension Cliffhangers © 2008 by Tom Conklin, Scholastic Teaching Resources